Ancient History of India

Up to 10th Century A.D.

Ancient History of India

Up to 10th Century A.D.

Atlantic Research Division

ATLANTIC
PUBLISHERS & DISTRIBUTORS (P) LTD

Published by

ATLANTIC

PUBLISHERS & DISTRIBUTORS (P) LTD

7/22, Ansari Road, Darya Ganj,
New Delhi-110002
Phones : +91-11-40775252, 23273880, 23275880, 23280451
Fax : +91-11-23285873
Web : www.atlanticbooks.com
E-mail : orders@atlanticbooks.com

Branch Office
5, Nallathambi Street, Wallajah Road,
Chennai-600002
Phones : +91-44-64611085, 32413319
E-mail : chennai@atlanticbooks.com

Printed in India at Glorious Printers, A-13, D.S.I.D.C.,
Jhilmil Industrial Area, Delhi-110095

Preface

Ancient history of India is hugely magnificent, affluent and diverse. It begins with Stone Age, which is a broad prehistoric time with no clear geographical demarcation. The remains of the *Homo erectus* in Hathnora in the Narmada Valley in central India indicate that India was inhabited since the Middle Pleistocene era. The Mesolithic Period also saw the permanent settlements in the Rock Shelters of Bhimbetka in what today constitutes the state of Madhya Pradesh. Neolithic culture emerged in South Asia and flourished in the Western parts of Indian subcontinent. Bronze Age in India started with the Indus Valley Civilization, the remains of which are found in modern day India in some cities of Gujarat, Haryana, Rajasthan, as well as in Sindh and Punjab in Pakistan.

Ancient India was the meeting ground of the East and the West and subject to innumerable invasions from various parts of the world. At that time, its natural isolation and appealing religious doctrines and social norms allowed it to adapt to and absorb people of many races who penetrated its Northern mountain passes. Although Greeks, Persians, Chinese, Arabs, Portuguese, British and other invaders had their way with the land, yet the local Hindu kingdoms invariably survived their ravage, and managed to live out their own sagas of conquest and collapse.

Archaeological excavations in the North-eastern parts of India have evidenced a highly developed urban civilization in ancient India. Harappa and Mohenjodaro, two of its great cities, point out that Indus Valley Civilization was one of the oldest civilizations of ancient India.

The Aryans migrated into the Indian subcontinent from the North-west and settled in the Saptasindhu region while adapting to the prevailing Indian culture. It was around 2nd century BC, and in the ancient history of India, it is known as the Vedic Civilization. The Aryans lived in tribes and spoke Sanskrit, which was a part of Indo-European group of languages. They intermingled with the locals and the history of India during this time witnessed the rise of major kingdoms known as Mahajanapadas. It was followed by the Mauryan empire, the Sunga, Kanva and Andhara dynasties, then the Guptas and their successors, the most important of whom was Harsha Vardhana.

India, from time immemorial has been the centre of world activities. Its civilization is among the oldest of world civilizations along with Mesopotamia and Ancient Egypt. However, the sources are too slight to accurately reconstruct the ancient Indian history. Different writers and scholars—both Indian and foreign—have expressed different views about various aspects of ancient history of India. Therefore, it becomes difficult for a learner to come to definite conclusions. The aim of this book is to present clear views on all the pertinent areas of the subject. This has been done by explaining the historical facts about ancient Indian history upto 10th century AD, and synthesizing the views of well-established historians worldwide. Only those views have been dwelt upon which have been widely accepted by historians and experts. Events and facts have been described in a simple language and lucid manner for easy comprehension by the readers.

The book covers the syllabi of B.A. (Hons) and B.A. (Prog) in History prescribed by Delhi University and will be helpful to the students pursuing these courses. As the syllabus for graduation is more or less the same in every university, the book will cater to the needs of students of History all over India. Besides, it will benefit those preparing for various competitive examinations with History as a subject.

Atlantic Research Division

Contents

Physical Features of India

1

Introduction

Physical features of a country influence its history up to a great extent. India is a vast country and Indian civilization is among the most ancient civilizations of the world. Besides, it occupies a place of pride in the history of cultures and civilizations of the world. There are five countries in the subcontinent—India, Pakistan, Bangladesh, Nepal and Bhutan. India is the largest among them and it comprises twenty-eight states and six Union Territories. According to the 2001 Census, the population of India is over one hundred crores. India is a geographical unit in the shape of two triangles joined together. On the north-east and north-west are the Great Himalayan Mountains and on the other side are the major seas, i.e. the Arabian Sea on the west, the Bay of Bengal on the east and the Indian Ocean on the south. In spite of the natural boundaries, India never remained in isolation. She has maintained unbroken contact with all civilized countries of the world. This was facilitated by her position in the midst of the Indian Ocean and her early cultural advancement.

The history of a country is determined by two factors. They are (i) Human factor and (ii) Environmental or Geographical factor. Physically, India is divided into three well-marked divisions:

The Great Mountain Wall—The Himalayas

Physically and intellectually, India has been greatly influenced by the Himalayas. These are approximately 2400 kilometres long. These ranges have not only checked invasions but have also protected us from the cold winds coming from the north. They also stop the monsoon winds from the seas which result in rainfall in the northern plains. However, there are some mountain passes which, though difficult, have provided access to determined invaders, traders and missioners. These have helped greatly in cultural intermixing in ancient times. Some of these passes are Gomal, Bolan, and Khyber passes. The Aryans, Persians, Kushans, Parthians, Hunas, Turks and Mughals came to India through these north-western passes. Likewise, Buddhism and other Indian elements were carried out to Central Asia and Afghanistan through these mountain passes. The Himalayas gave three important rivers, the Indus, the Ganges, and the Brahmaputra. These river systems helped in the growth of important civilization in the early times.

The Great Northern Plains

The northern plains are very fertile and prosperous land. Due to its richness, it has been the centre of foreign invasions. All important dynasties developed and flourished here. The three important river systems make their region fertile. The Ganga-Yamuna doab region has continuously seen active cultural development since the ancient time. It is this region where *mahajanpadas* like Kosala, Kasi and Magadha were established in the 6th century B.C. The two main religions of India, Jainism and Buddhism, also took birth here. The lower Gangetic plains constitute the Bengal region. The Tamralipti or Tamluk was an important seaport of this region which played a significant role in commercial activities. In the west India, the most important sea port is Bharuch (Broach). The great Northern Plain always remained the pivot of the political cultural life of the country.

The Great Deccan Plateau

Peninsular India includes the Deccan plateau and the coastal plains of south India. The term Deccan, sometimes, is extended so as to cover the whole of India south of the Narmada; but is usually understood as designating a more limited territory, in which Malabar and the Tamil countries of the extreme south are not included. Thus, limited the term signifies the whole region occupied by the Telugu speaking populations, as well as Maharashtra, or the Maratha country. The Deccan is to the south of the Vindhya and Satpura ranges. The Deccan plateau is geologically the oldest part of India. Its sides are formed by the Western and Eastern Ghats. These are hilly terrains. At the southern end of the Western Ghats is the Palghat pass which linked the west coast to the Kaveri valley and played an important role in the Indo-Roman trade in ancient time. The Eastern Ghats merge more gradually into the plateau and the coastal plain. The coastal plains constitute the states of Tamil Nadu in east and Kerala in west. This region witnessed the flourishing of the Sangam culture in the ancient times. The ports such as Arikamedu and Kaveripattinam gave impetus to the Indo-Roman Trade in early centuries of Christian era. The Tamil region evolved a distinct linguistic and cultural identity of its own. The Deccan plateau played an important part in the course of Indian history. It served as a safety zone for the culture of the north. Whenever the Hindus were persecuted by the Muslim rulers in the north, they slipped away to the south and saved their culture, literature and religion.

Effects on Political History

India is colossal in size. The country is almost as large as the whole of the continent of Europe excluding Russia. The physical features of India have separated it from other Asian countries. It is cut off from the rest of the Asia by the high wall of the Himalayas. It is due to Himalayas that we have ignored the defence of our country. It served as a great natural defence to the people of India. Many important dynasties developed and flourished in our plains. The most notable of rulers in the earliest time cherished the ambition of universal Indian dominion, and severally attained it in a greater or less degree. Not one of them, however, attained it completely, and this failure involves a lack of unity in political history which renders the task of the historian difficult. The Vindhya Mountains have divided India into two parts. Hence, due to the disintegrating influences of natural physical divisions, racial distinctions and diversity of language, manners and customs, complete political unification could not be achieved until the establishment of British sovereignty; still India possesses a deep fundamental unity. The vastness and prosperity of the country provided an ample scope for the adventurous rulers to fulfil their imperialistic designs. The names of Samudra Gupta and Alauddin Khilji can be mentioned in this connection.

Effects on Cultural History

In the 5th century B.C. Herodotus observed that "of all the nations that we know, it is India which has the largest population". This large group of human population is comprised of several ethnic groups, split up into countless castes, admitting various creeds. These distinct castes and creeds value different culture according to the physical features of their areas. Geography of India not only influenced the political but also the cultural history of India. The north and south developed different types of civilization. In the field of culture, the contribution of "North India" is supreme. The wealth and development of this region made the people peace and ease loving. Free from the worries of livelihood, they had enough time for the cultivation of art and literature. The Vedic Literature is the most valuable treasure of our country. The art and architecture under Mauryas and Guptas, the Gandhara Artunder Kushans, the establishment of Nalanda and Taxila universities are considered as cultural effect of Geography on History. Life in the south was safe and secure as compared to the north. As a result, south proved to be the defence of Indian civilization and culture at a time when the north had to face the attacks of foreign invaders. The absence of transport and communication created many difficulties in those days in India. So trade and commerce contracted considerably. During the Gupta period, Indian trade and commerce was at its prime and it was due to the establishment of certain colonies abroad that India was termed as 'Greater India'.

India—A Land of Unity in Diversity

As we know that physical features of a country greatly influence the course of its history. India is situated in the south of the Asian continent. India has a separate individuality of its own. Nature has given her a geographical unity by separating it from the rest of the world. Her type of civilization has too many features which differentiate it from that of all other regions of the world, while they are common to the whole country, or rather subcontinent, in a degree sufficient to justify its treatment as a unit in the history of the social, religious, and intellectual development of mankind. The diversity of Indian history is the outcome of its natural physical divisions. The vast area of the country and unsuitable communication were great handicaps in the way of political unification of the country. The foreign immigrants poured into the north through the mountain passes of the north-west. The pre-Aryans, the Indo-Aryans, the Greeks, the Scythians, the Hunas, the Turks, etc., made India their home. Each ethnic group contributed its might to the making of Indian culture. All these people mixed up so indistinguishably with each other that none of them can be identified in their original form even up to this date. Different cultures blended with one another through the ages. Many pre-Aryan or Dravidian terms occur in the Vedic texts. Similarly, many Pali and Sanskrit terms appear in the Sangam literature.

Since ancient times, India has been the land of several religions. Ancient India witnessed the birth of Hinduism, Jainism and Buddhism. Although Indian people speak different languages, practice different religions, and observe different social customs, they follow certain common styles of life throughout the country. Therefore, our country shows a deep underlying unity in spite of great diversity. The great epics, *Ramayana* and *Mahabharata* are honoured by people all over India. Originally composed in Sanskrit, these epics came to be presented in different local languages. Although the Indian cultural values and ideas were expressed in different forms, the substance remained the same throughout the country. The social customs are almost the same among the great variety of Indian people which binds them together. The stories of our natural heroes like Ram and Krishna are heard with equal devotion all over India. Hence, India has emerged a multi-religious and multi-cultural society.

In fact, the ancients exert for unity. They looked upon this vast subcontinent as one land. The name *Bharatavarsha* or the land of *Bharata* was given to the whole country, after the name of an ancient tribe called the *Bharatas*. Our ancient poets, scholars, and writers viewed the country as an integral unit. This kind of political unity was attained at least twice during the Mauryan and Gupta Empires. The unity of India was also recognized by foreigners. They first came into contact with the people living on the Sindhu or the Indus, and so they named the whole country after this river. The word *Hind* is derived from the Sanskrit term *Sindhu* (the Sanskrit word *Sindhu* means river, stream or ocean, it is attested 176 times in the Rigveda), and in course of time the country came to be known as 'India' in Greek, and 'Hind' in Persian and Arabic languages.

IMPORTANT QUESTIONS

1. How far geographical regions and environment have influenced the course of early Indian history?
2. Write a note on the effect of physical features on cultural history of India.
3. Unity in diversity has been regarded as one of the basic features of the Indian culture. Do you think that the geographical conditions of India, in anyway, are responsible for it?

REFERENCES

Chaurasia, R.S., *History of Ancient India*, New Delhi: Atlantic Publishers, 2008.

Directorate of School Education, *Higher Secondary Textbook of Tamil Nadu*.

Jayapalan, N., *History of India*, New Delhi: Atlantic Publishers, 2001.

Jha, D.N., *Ancient India*, Delhi, 1998.

Raychaudhuri, H.C. (Dr.), *An Advanced History of India*, New Delhi: Macmillan Publishers India Limited, 1978.

Thapar, Romila, *Early India from the Origins to AD. 1300*, New Delhi, Penguin Books, 2002.

Sources of Ancient Indian History

2

Introduction

The study of past happenings is known as *History*. Its study helps us to reconstruct the past to understand the processes that enabled the early man to successfully conquer their environment and develop the present-day civilization. We can know about our ancestors and also learn from their experiences to lead our lives. Many of the ancient civilizations are now either extinct or have failed to preserve their past traditions. The Indian civilization, on the other hand, is not only a living civilization of the world but has been significant. We have abundant sources for the reconstruction of Indian History. From these sources we get immense information about the Indian society during various periods. The sources of the early history of India may be arranged in two classes: Literary and Archaeological. Literary sources of India are partly sacred (including Brahmanical, Jain and Buddhist texts) and partly secular (including accounts of Megasthenes, Fa-Hien, Ptolemy, I-tsing, etc.) in nature. The accounts of foreigners supplement our knowledge of the early history of India. Archaeological sources include inscriptions, coins, monuments, paintings and sculptures. Let us see these sources under the following headings:

Religious Literature

Most of the ancient Indian literature is of religious character. The literary sources can be further sub-divided into three groups, viz. Brahmanical, Jain and Buddhist.

The earliest group of literature is the Vedic literature. The four Vedas, i.e. Rig, Yajur, Sama and Atharva Vedas give a graphic picture of the Aryans. A critical study of the Rig Vedic literature will throw a flood of light on the history of early Aryans in India, and the study of rest three Vedas will tell us about the social, economic, religious and political life of the later Aryans. *Upanishads* contain philosophical discussions.

The great epics, *Ramayana* of Valmiki and *Mahabharata* of Ved Vyas are regarded as legends. They furnish us with a true picture of the economic, social and political conditions of the later Aryans. They for the first time throw light on the dark corners of history.

The history of origin of dynasties in ancient India is known from the *Puranas*. Although the *Puranas* have certain shortcomings as the real history is mixed up with folklores, it is highly reliable. According to V.A. Smith, "Five out of the eighteen works of this class, namely, the *Vayu*, *Matsya*, *Vishnu*, *Brahmanda*, and *Bhagavata* contain such lists. The *Matsya* is the earliest and the most authoritative. Modern European writers have been inclined to disparage unduly the authority of the Puranic lists, but closer study finds in them much genuine and valuable historical tradition."

The religious books of the Jains and Buddhists refer to historical persons and incidents connected with their respective religions. The Buddhist texts including *Jataka*, or birth stories of Buddha and *Tripitakas* refer to the political condition of India in the fifth and sixth centuries B.C. The *Jatakas* also refer to the social and economic conditions of the period between the fifth and second centuries B.C. The earliest Buddhist texts were written in *Pali*. The sacred books of the Jain sect are written in Prakrit, are still very imperfectly known, also contain numerous historical statements and allusions of considerable value. The Jain literature mainly consists of *Angas* and *Upaangas*. They contain the philosophical concepts of the Jains.

Secular Literature

The category of literature that does not contain religion as its theme is known as secular literature. It includes biographies, law books, etc. The *Arthasastra* of Kautilya provides important material for the study of Indian economy and polity during

Mauryan period. Panini's *Ashtadhyayi* is the earliest and the most important work on grammar. It is dated to 700 B.C. The works of Kalidas comprising poems and dramas give a insight of social and cultural life of the Guptas. Important works of Kalidas are *Abhijananashakuntalam, Ritusamhara* and *Meghadutam*. Often court poets used to write biographies in praise of their patrons. One such account is *Harshacharita* of Banabhatta. In this we do not find the mention of defeat of Harsha by Chalukya King Pulakesin II. But the inscriptions of Pulakesin II claim a victory over Harsha. In this case, it can be noticed that Banabhatta deliberately did not mention the defeat of his patron. The three dramas of Harsha, the *Nagananda*, the *Ratnavali* and the *Priyadarsika* throw interesting light on the history of the 7th century A.D. For the history of Kashmir we have the most important chronicle *Rajatrangini* by Kalhana. It was written in 12th century A.D. It gives an authentic account of history of Kashmir. The earliest south Indian literature is called Sangam literature. It was written in Tamil and is secular in nature. The literature consists of short and long poems in praise of various heroes. The Sangam literature is our major source for the study of south Indian society, economy and polity from 300 B.C. to 300 A.D.

Foreign Accounts

Foreign accounts also give a lot of information about the Indian history. *Indica* of Magasthenes, the ambassador of Selukus at the court of Chandra Gupta is of high historical value. The *Periplus of the Erythrean Sea* and Ptolemy's *Geography,* both in Greek, provide valuable data about the trade between India and the Roman Empire during the first and second centuries.

Fa-Hein, who visited India during Chandra Gupta II reign, provided useful information about the governance of that period. Hiuen Tsang book *Si-Yu-Ki* has been most helpful for the reconstruction of history during the time of Harshavardhana. Hiuen Tsang also describes in detail the glory of Nalanda University. The observations of I-tsing are primarily religious in character. He travelled in India from 671 A.D. to 695 A.D. The importance of the Chinese accounts lies in the fact that they are contemporary and dated records.

The learned mathematician and astronomer, Alberuni who came to India with Mahmud of Ghazni early in the eleventh century has written a truly useful account *Tarikh-i-Hind*. According to V.A. Smith, "It is of high value as an account of Hindu manners, science, and literature; but contributes comparatively little information which can be utilized for the purposes of political history."

Archaeological

Archaeology is the science that enables us to systematically dig the successive layers of old mounds and to form an idea of the material life of the people of the past on the basis of remains found there. Study of archaeology can be further divided into the following categories:

(i) Inscriptions

Inscriptions are permanent writings engraved on hard surface. Study of inscriptions on rocks, pillars, temple walls, caves, seals, copper plates, etc. is known as Epigraphy. Inscriptions have proved a source of great significance for the reconstruction of history of ancient India. Their object was mainly to commemorate a great event. The inscriptions are useful in fixing dates and often regulate and supplement other sources. The majority of inscriptions were written in Brahmi script from left to right. Asoka's edicts, or sermons on stone, form a class by themselves. The Iron Pillar at Mehrauli tells about Chandra Gupta. The Allahabad Pillar Inscription describes the career and achievements of Samudragupta. The Hathigumpha Cave Inscription gives a graphic picture about Kharavela of Kalinga. Sometimes foreign inscriptions too lend us aid. The Boghaz Koi (Asia Minor) inscriptions which mention Vedic gods testify to the movements of Aryan tribes.

(ii) Numismatics (Coins)

Like the inscriptions, the study of the Indian coins also enlightens us a great deal regarding the history of ancient India. Coins provide useful information regarding economic history as they were used as a medium of exchange. They are of various metals—gold, silver, copper and bronze. The name of the king with imperial titles can be gathered from those coins. The earliest coins found in India contained certain symbols and were called punched marked coins. They date back to sixth century B.C. onwards and were made up of silver and copper. We get a lot of information from the coins about the Indo-Bactrians and Kushan Kings. From the coins of Guptas, we know the economic condition of their period. Some coins also throw light on the personality of a ruler like the coins during Samudragupta's reign. Vehicle of Vishnu inscribed on some coins indicate that Samudragupta was a devotee of that deity. Veena attest his love for music. From the Roman coins, we get a lot of information regarding the trade and commerce that existed between India and Rome. The discovery of the same kind of coins at different places helps us in fixing the extent of various kingdoms in ancient India.

(iii) Architecture

The monumental class of archaeological evidence is considered by itself of high illustrative value. It greatly helps in realizing the power and magnificence of some of the ancient dynasties. The temples, the stupas, and the monasteries brightly depict the artistic achievements and religious devotion of the people and the rulers.

(iv) Sculpture

In the Indian subcontinent, the first sculpture dates back to the Indus Valley Civilization, where stone and bronze carvings have been discovered. Later, as Hinduism, Buddhism and Jainism developed further, India produced some of the most intricate bronzes in the world, as well as unrivaled temple carvings. Different school of sculpture developed in different regions, viz. Amravati, Mathura, Gandhara, school of art from third century B.C till second century A.D. We know certain historical facts from the sculptures.

(v) Painting

The history of art in ancient India begins with prehistoric rock paintings. Such rock paintings can be seen in the Bhimbetaka paintings, belonging to the prehistoric age. Cave paintings of India date back to the prehistoric times. The finest examples of these paintings—comprise the murals of Ajanta, Ellora, Bagh, Sittanavasal, etc. which reflect an emphasis on naturalism. Ancient cave paintings of India serve as a window to our ancestors, who used to inhabit these caves.

IMPORTANT QUESTIONS

1. How far the archaeological excavations over the decades have added to our knowledge on early India?
2. Give the importance of secular literature in knowing the ancient Indian history.
3. Examine the importance of coins and epigraphs as sources for the reconstruction of early Indian history.

REFERENCES

Chaurasia, R.S., *History of Ancient India*, New Delhi: Atlantic Publishers, 2008.

Jayapalan, N., *History of India*, New Delhi: Atlantic Publishers, 2001.

Jha, D.N., *Ancient India*, Delhi, 1998.

National Institute of Open Learning, *E notes*.

Sharma, L.P., *History of Ancient India,* New Delhi: Konark Publishers, 1996.

Smith, V.A., *The Early History of India,* New Delhi: Atlantic Publishers, 1999.

Thaper, Romila, *Early India From the Origins to A.D. 1300*, New Delhi, Penguin Books, 2002.

Prehistoric India

3

Introduction

Man had lived on this earth for millions of years before he learned the art of writing. This long distant past when man kept no written records is called pre-history. The prehistoric period in the history of mankind can roughly be calculated from 200000 B.C. to about 3500 B.C. As they could not develop the art of writing their history can be traced from the tools they used for various purposes and other archeological excavations.

On the basis of tools used the prehistoric period can be divided into three phases: Paleolithic (from unknown till 10000 B.C.); Mesolithic (10000-8000 B.C.); and Neolithic (8000-3500 B.C.).

Paleolithic Age

The term has been derived from the Greek word 'paleo', which means old and 'lithic', meaning stone. Therefore, the term *Paleolithic Age* refers to the *Old Stone Age*. This name is applied to the earliest people, as the only evidence of their existence is furnished by a number of rude stone implements. It is now generally held that the earliest traces of human beings in India are found in the Punjab in the region between the Sindhu and Jhelum rivers. Men of this age did not know the use of metals, had no idea of cultivation and probably, did not know how to produce fire. They could not even make pottery. The main tools of Paleolithic phase were handaxes, cleavers and choppers. These tools were rough, undressed and heavy and were made by chipping the sides of the stones, mainly of hard rock called *quartzite*. From this fact, the Paleolithic men in

India are also known as *Quartzite men*. Gradually, sharper and less heavy tools came to be made. These tools were used for hunting, cutting, digging and other purposes.

In the beginning of this age, men did not know the use of cloth and remained naked, however, later they started covering their bodies with animal skins and tree-leaves. They neither buried nor burnt their dead bodies but left them as it is. The Paleolithic people practiced hunting and food-gathering for their subsistence. They led a nomadic life and migrated to different places in search of food. They lived on the flesh of animals and such fruits and vegetables as grew wild in jungles. However, they lived in groups to protect themselves from wild animals. They lived in natural shelters. Important sites of this age are: the Kashmir valley and the Sohan valley in Rawalpindi (now in Pakistan); Nevasa on a tributary of Godavari (in Maharashtra); Bhimbetka (near Bhopal) and Adamgarh in Madhya Pradesh and Belan valley (the region from Allahabad to Varanasi) in Uttar Pradesh.

The Paleolithic Age in India is divided into three phases, based on tool technology. These phases are:

(i) **Lower Paleolithic**: The main tool types in this phase were handaxes and cleavers, along with chopper-chopping tools. They were rough and heavy. The butt end of the handaxes was broader and the working edge is narrow.

(ii) **Middle Paleolithic**: The middle Paleolithic tools technology is characterized basically by the flake tool industry. The tools are made on flakes obtained by striking them out from pebbles or cobbles. Main tool was scraper.

(iii) **Upper Paleolithic**: The middle Paleolithic culture slowly evolved into the upper Palaeolithic culture.

This age continued up to 10000 B.C. It has been suggested that the Paleolithic men belonged to the Negrito race, like the modern people of the Andaman Islands, and were characterized by short stature, dark skin, woolly hair and flat noses.

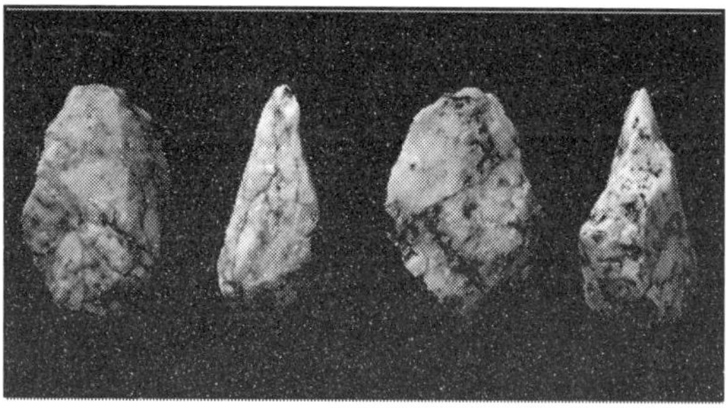

Palaeolithic tools

Mesolithic Age

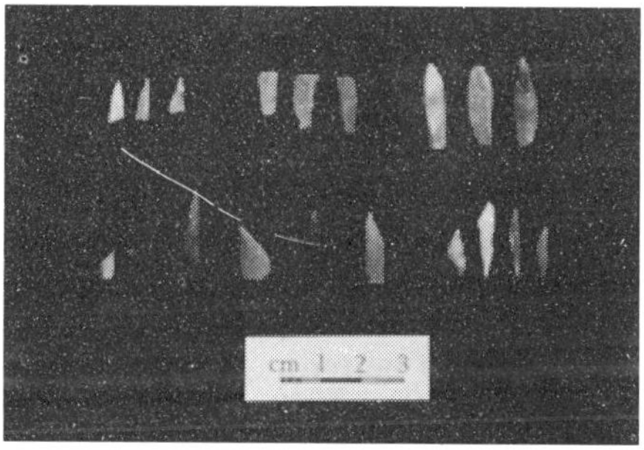

Mesolithic tools

The term is comprised of two words, *meso* and *lithic*. In Greek 'meso' means the middle and 'lithic' means stone. Hence, the *Mesolithic stage* of prehistory is also known as the *Middle Stone Age*. It was the transitional phase between the Paleolithic and the Neolithic Ages. In this age, men begin to make some progress in the field of their implements as well as in living. Men yet depended on fruits, fish and animal for their living and built no houses. But men started to bury their dead and the dog became their tamed animal. Mesolithic phase is marked by the important practice of domesticating animals. The main tools of this age are called microliths or small stone tools. The *microliths* were very small in size varying in lengths from 1 to 8 centimetres. They were fixed or tied in other objects to form an arrow or a spear. Some of these tools have geometric shapes as triangles, lunates and trapezes. Paleolithic and Mesolithic people practiced painting, of which evidence comes from Bhimbetka, Azamgarh, Pratapgarh and Mirzapur. These sites provide unquestionable testimony for the Mesolithic art which provides evidence of hunting, food gathering, fishing and other human activities like sexual union, childbirth and burial and thus gives a good idea of social, economic and other activities of the people. Animals like boar, buffalo, monkey and nilgai are often depicted in these paintings. This period continued upto 8000 B.C.

Neolithic Age

In Greek, 'Neo' stands for 'new'. Thus, the term 'neolithic age' refers to the *New Stone Age*. This was the last phase of prehistory. The term 'Neolithic' was coined by Jonn Lubbock. It was a period of primitive technological and social developments. The chief characteristic of this age was the new type of sharpened and polished stone tools. Neolithic period included different types of axes called 'celt'. Besides the stone tools, the sites of this period have also yielded various types of bone objects such as needles, scrapers, borers, arrowheads, pendants, bangles and earrings. This period also marked the beginning of agricultural practices and the domestication of animals. The people cultivated various kinds of crops such as wheat, barley, rice, millet, lentils, etc. The new polished tools made it easier for humans to cultivate, hunt and perform other activities in a better manner. It led to greater availability of food resources as well as to an increase in population, which in turn resulted in the increase in the number of village settlements. The dead body was buried and at times put in a large urn. Many of these urns have been found intact under the ground.

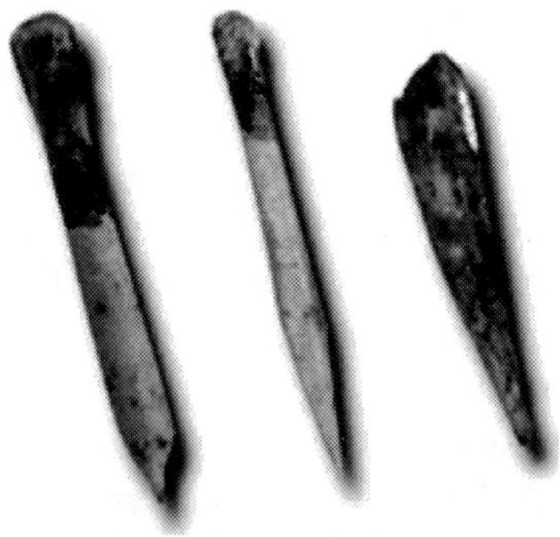

Bone tools of Neolithic age

Neolithic men abandoned wandering and led a settled life. They built houses, cooked their food and made clay pottery. We have found a rich collection of pottery from Malabar. Probably, they built the potter's wheel also. They also painted and decorated their pottery. Man of this age could spin and weave cotton and wool cloth. They had also started to think about religion and worship of gods and devils. He worshipped nature. The Neolithic cultures created the conditions which helped in the growth of towns in the later period. The remains of Neolithic men are found in almost every part of India. An ancient factory for the manufacture of stone implements has been discovered in the Bellary district, Madras, where we can still trace the various stages of their construction. The main Neolithic sites are Mehrgarh in Baluchistan; Burzahom and Gufkral in Kashmir valley; Chirand in Bihar and Belan valley in Uttar Pradesh. Miles Burkitt put forward the following four characteristics of a culture to be called a Neolithic Culture:

(i) Agriculture practice
(ii) Domestication of animals
(iii) Polished and grinned stone tools
(iv) Pottery manufacture

Dolmen

The Neolithic Age is also characterized by megalithic tombs or dolmens, usually consisting of three or more upright stones supporting a large flat horizontal capstone. Most date from the early Neolithic period (4000 to 3000 B.C.E.). Dolmens were usually covered with earth or smaller stones to form a barrow, though in many cases that covering has weathered away, leaving only the stone "skeleton" of the burial mound intact. These dolmens are one of the most common megalithic structures of Neolithic Age all over the world. It is often assumed that dolmens were constructed for cremation purposes. However, the absence of human remains in several prominent dolmens, combined with certain construction features suggests that this can no longer be considered a definitive theory. These Megaliths were, in most cases, located outside the settlement area. These have also yielded the first iron objects from south India. Nagpur region in Maharashtra to the southern tip of the Indian Peninsula has yielded large number of Megaliths.

Neolithic Food Revolution

The Neolithic Revolution was the first agricultural revolution. It was the transition from hunting and gathering to agriculture and settlement. Archaeological data indicates that various forms of plants and animal domestication evolved independently during 8000-5000 B.C. However, the Neolithic Revolution involved far more than the adoption of a limited set of food-producing techniques. During the next millennia, it transformed the small and mobile groups of hunter-gatherers that had hitherto dominated human history into sedentary societies based in built-up villages and towns, which radically modified their natural environment by means of specialized food-crop cultivation (e.g. irrigation and food storage technologies) that allowed extensive surplus food production. These developments provided the basis for high population density settlements, specialized and complex labour diversification, trading economies, the development of non-portable art, architecture, and culture, centralized administrations and political structures, and writing system. The relationship of the above-mentioned Neolithic characteristics to the onset of agriculture, their sequence of emergence, and empirical relation to each other at various Neolithic sites remain the subject of academic debate, and seem to vary from place to place, rather than being the outcome of universal laws of social evolution.

Wheat and barley were the earliest cereals grown. As a result man began to settle down in certain selected areas. This led to the growth of villages and farming communities. The tools he needed also changed. All these developments took place first in north-western India and culminated in the rise and growth of great Indus Civilization while the rest of the Indian subcontinent was late in undergoing the transition from Mesolithic to the Neolithic and then to the Chalcolithic periods.

Rock Art

Rock art is a term used in archaeology for any human-made markings made on natural stone. They can be divided into: Petroglyphs carvings into stone surfaces, pictographs rock and cave paintings. The rock paintings were an important and distinct feature of the Mesolithic people, though their beginning may be traced to the upper Paleolithic period. These paintings are made on the walls of rock shelters, maximum of which have been found at Bhimbetka in Madhya Pradesh.

The Bhimbetka rock art sites are about 45 kilometres south-east of Bhopal. They are the ones that are always mentioned whenever Indian rock art is alluded to. The rock shelters and caves of Bhimbetka have a number of interesting paintings which throw light on the social and economic life of Mesolithic people. The main objects of paintings are hunting, fishing, food gathering, scenes of childbirth, communal dancing and drinking, and religious rites and burials, as well as the natural environment around them. Animals like boar, buffalo, monkey and nilgai are often depicted in these paintings. On the walls hundreds of images, very often superimposed upon one another, constitute a fantastic canvas that has been many times reused to paint white and red figures. The abundance of scenes of all sorts in Indian rock art is one of its major and most appealing characteristics.

In addition to animals, there are human figures and hunting scenes, giving a clear picture of the weapons they used: barbed spears, pointed sticks, bows and arrows. It is certain that the sites with paintings and/or engravings are exceptionally numerous all over the country, particularly in its centre. Thus, we can conclude that Mesolithic society was more stable than the one in Paleolithic age, though hunting, gathering still remained its main preoccupation.

Depiction of animals and humans, Rock Shelters of Bhimbetka, *Courtesy* ASI

Disparities do exist according to the areas. However, "in spite of the great distances of the different regions Indian rock paintings bear surprising affinity in forms, subject matters and design elements to their contemporaries". Among the colours used red is overwhelmingly dominant at all periods. It comes from iron oxides such as haematite. White (from white clay like kaolin) has also been widely used. Other colours are scarcer, like "green and yellow derived from copper minerals" or "blue or coal black obtained from manganese or charcoal". Painting was carried out by rubbing the colour nodule dry, or with water, without any visible use of organic binding material, using fingertips or twigs. The subjects represented are quite varied and numerous. Depending on the periods and the areas, their relative proportions may change hugely. For example, animals, as we have seen, are less abundant at some Bhimbetka sites than in the Chambal valley and humans are central to historic paintings.

The Age of Metals

The Neolithic or New Stone Age lasted until around 4000 B.C. During this period, remarkable progress has been made by human beings in the field of science, technology and culture in general. After many centuries, the Neolithic man in India learnt the use of metals. Stone was superseded by iron. But in the beginning axes, swords, spearheads and other implements were made of copper. It was in turn followed by bronze and iron. When the use of these metals became general, the period was known as the Iron and Copper ages. Gold was used for ornaments only. The Bronze period intervened between the Neolithic and Iron ages. Bronze is a good substitute for copper, as it is harder than copper and is more suitable for the manufacture of tools and weapons. Bronze implements of early times have been found in India along with those of copper, but it does not appear that metal was ever generally used in India to the exclusion of copper. In other words, there was, properly speaking, no Bronze Age in India.

IMPORTANT QUESTIONS

1. Highlight the salient features of the Paleolithic and Mesolithic cultures of India.
2. Write a note on the prehistoric rock art of India.
3. Examine the geographical distribution and subsistence pattern of the Neolithic cultures of India.
4. Discuss the tool-technology and subsistence pattern during the Paleolithic and Mesolithic periods in India.

REFERENCES

Chaurasia, R.S., *History of Ancient India*, New Delhi: Atlantic Publishers, 2008.

Jayapalan, N., *History of India*, New Delhi: Atlantic Publishers, 2001.

Jha, D.N., *Ancient India*, Delhi, 1998.

Majumdar, R.C. (Dr.), *An Advanced History of India*, New Delhi: Macmillan Publishers, 1978.

National Institute of Open Learning, *E notes*.

Sharma, L.P., *History of Ancient India*, New Delhi: Konark Publishers, 1996.

Thaper, Romila, *Early India From the Origins to A.D. 1300*, New Delhi, Penguin Books, 2002.

Indus Valley Civilization

4

Introduction

We have learnt that the people in prehistoric times used tools and weapons made of stone. Later man started using metals. Copper was the first metal to be used by man for making tools. Gradually, several cultures developed in Indian subcontinent which were based on the use of stone and copper tools. They also used bronze, a mixture of copper and tin, for this purpose. This phase in history is known as the Chalcolithic (chalco means copper; lithic means stone) period. The brightest chapter in the Chalcolithic period in India is the Harappan civilization which is also referred to as the Indus Valley Civilization.

Today, it is also termed as the Harappan civilization because Harappa was the first site, which brought to light the presence of this civilization. Besides, recent archaeological findings indicate that this civilization was spread much beyond the Indus Valley. Therefore, it is better to be called as the Harappan civilization. Our knowledge of the life and culture of the Harappan people is based only on the archaeological excavations as the script of that period has not been deciphered so far.

The Harappan civilization did not appear all of a sudden. It developed gradually from earlier Neolithic village cultures. It is believed that the better technology to exploit the fertile plains of river Indus might have resulted in increased agricultural production. This led to the production of larger surplus to feed and maintain, non-agricultural people such as artisans, administrators, etc. It also helped in the promotion of exchange or trading contacts with distant regions. It brought prosperity to the Harappan people and they were able to set up cities.

By around 2000 B.C. several regional cultures developed in different parts of the subcontinent which were also based on the use of stone and copper tools. These Chalcolithic cultures which lay outside the Harappan zone were not so rich and flourishing. These were basically rural in nature. The origin and development of these cultures is placed in the chronological span between circa 2000 B.C. and 700 B.C. These are found in Western and Central India and described as non-Harappan Chalcolithic cultures.

Origin

There has been much controversy among scholars regarding the race to which the Harappan people belonged. Different views have been expressed mainly on the basis of human skeletons and skulls found in the ruins. While some scholars have come to the conclusion that they were Dravidians, others are of the view that they were the same as Sumerians. According to Sir John Marshall, the Indus civilization was quite different from the earlier vedic civilization. According to him, while the Aryans were worshippers of cow, the Indus people worshipped bull. The Aryans worshipped male deities and the Harappan people worshipped Mother Goddess. The Aryans were pastoral people and the Indus people were great traders. The people of Harappa had urban civilization and the Aryans were village people. There is also difference in the nature of weapons of both of them. The Aryans produced offensive weapons and were great warriors. They used long swords and horses for fighting. On the contrary, the Indus people were peace loving and hence produced defensive weapons. They did not even know horse-riding.

Settlement Patterns

In 1924, Sir John Marshall, the then Director-General of Archaeology with the help of R.D. Banerjee and R.D. Dayaram Sahni made extensive excavations at Mohenjodaro and Harappa. Harappa is situated on the banks of the river Ravi in the Montgomery district of West Punjab (now in Pakistan). Mohenjodaro is situated at a distance of about 200 miles north of Karachi in the Larkana district of Sindh. These and other minor excavations at various other sites in Sindh, Baluchistan such as Chanhudaro, Naal, etc. have proved beyond doubt that some 5000 years ago a highly civilized community flourished in these regions.

The Indus valley civilization has been kept under pre-history as the Indus people, though evolved a script, it has not been deciphered. The Indus Valley Civilization was a Bronze Age Civilization (3300-1500 B.C.) that was located in the north-western region of the Indian subcontinent consisting of what is now mainly modern-day Pakistan and north-west India. Flourishing around the Indus river basin, the civilization primarily centred along the Indus and the Punjab region extending into the Ganga-Yamuna Doab. Geographically, the civilization was spread over an area of some 1,260,000 km^2, making it the largest ancient civilization in the world.

The Indus valley is one of the world's earliest urban civilizations, along with its contemporaries, Mesopotamia and Ancient Egypt. At its peak, the Indus civilization may have had a population of well over five million.

The Harappan civilization has been divided into three phases: Early Harappa (3300-2600 B.C.)—it was marked by some town-planning in the form of mud structures, elementary trade, etc., Mature Harappa (2600-1900 B.C.)—it was the period of well-developed towns with burnt brick structures, art and crafts, both inland and foreign trade; and Late Harappa (1900-1300 B.C.)—it was a period of gradual decay of the significant urban traits.

The mature phase of Indus valley civilization is known as the Harappan civilization, excavated in the 1920s in what was at the time the Punjab Province of British India (now in Pakistan). Excavation of Harappan sites have been ongoing since 1920, with important breakthroughs occurring as recently as 1999. To date, over 1,052 cities and settlements have been found, mainly in the general region of the Ghaggar-Hakra river and its tributaries. Among the settlements were the major urban centres of Harappa, Lothal, Mohenjodaro, Dholavira, Kalibanga, Rakhigarhi, Naal, and Ropar, etc. These excavations prove that this civilization flourished over a vast area comprising the whole of Sind and the Punjab, the bulk of Kathiwar,

Rajasthan, the valley of N.W.F.P. and the northern part of Gangetic basin.

Town Planning

The excavation work carried out at various sites has shown without doubt that the Indus valley people were primarily urban people. "These cities are the earliest", says Dr. Mackay, an authority on the subject, "yet they appear to be so modern". A sophisticated and technologically advanced urban culture is evident in the Indus valley civilization making them the first urban centres in the region. The quality of municipal town planning suggests the knowledge of urban planning and efficient municipal governments which placed a high priority on hygiene.

The houses were simple yet strong. The walls were thick and made up of burnt bricks. 'L' shaped bricks were occasionally used for corners. The bigger houses had many rooms surrounding a square courtyard. These houses were provided with private wells, kitchens and bathing platforms. Although some houses were larger than others, Indus civilization cities were remarkable for their apparent, if relative, egalitarianism. All the houses had access to water and drainage facilities. This gives the impression of a society with relatively low wealth concentration, though clear social levelling is seen in personal adornments.

The uniformity is noticed in the layout of the towns, streets, structure, brick size, drains, etc. Almost all the major sites (Harappa, Mohenjodaro, Kalibanga and others) are divided into two parts—a citadel on the higher mound on the western side and a lower town on the eastern side of the settlement. The citadel contains large structures which might have functioned as administrative or ritual centres. The residential buildings are built in the lower town. The streets were quite broad varying from 9 ft to 34 ft in breadth. The corners of the streets were rounded off perhaps to enable the heavy carts to take an easy turn. These streets intersected each other at right angles. And according to Dr. Mackay, "They were so arranged that the prevailing winds could work as a sort of suction-pump thereby clearing the atmosphere automatically." No building was allowed to encroach upon a public highway.

As seen in Harappa, Mohenjodaro and the recently excavated Rakhigarhi, the urban plan included the world's first known urban sanitation systems. Within the city, individual homes or groups of homes obtained water from wells. From a room that appears to have been set aside for bathing, waste-water was directed to covered drains, which lined the major streets. Houses opened to inner courtyards and smaller lanes. The drainage system of the Harappans was elaborate and well laid out. They constructed their drains on very scientific lines. The drains were made of gypsum, lime and mortar. Every house had drains, which opened into the street drains. These drains were covered with bricks or stone slabs and were provided with inspection traps and manholes at regular intervals for inspection. These elaborate drainage systems show that Harappan people had developed a high sense of health and sanitation.

The Indus people had constructed three types of buildings—dwelling houses, shrines or public halls, and public baths. Most of the houses were double storeyed. They were made of baked bricks and mud mortar. They had paved floor. There were doors, windows and ventilators. The roofs were made of mud, reed, and wood. Every house had its own wells, bathrooms, courtyards, drains and kitchens. A public building has also been discovered. It is a high pillared hall of 80 feet square, which was perhaps used as an assembly hall to transact the business of the state. Another such structure is the state-granary about 150 feet by 200 feet, which is further subdivided into smaller storage blocks of 50 feet by 20 feet each for storing different types of grains. But the most important building is the Great Bath (at Mohenjodaro) which still excites our curiosity after a lapse of about 5000 years. The pool is about 139 feet in length, 23 feet in breadth and 9 feet deep. It was perhaps used by the general public on festive days. This pool was provided with gallaries and rooms on all sides and also with a hamāms. It has a flight of steps at either end and was fed by a well nearby. Every attempt was made to make it strong and water-tight. Many thick layers of well-backed bricks laid in gypsum-mortar were joined together for the purpose of making the whole construction very strong. The solidarity of its construction is amply borne out of the fact that it has successfully withstood the ravages of time for full 5000 years. At Lothal, a brick structure has been identified as a dockyard meant for berthing ships and handling cargo. This suggests that Lothal was an important port and trading centre of the Harappan people. Thus, Indus valley civilization was a highly developed civilization.

Dr. A.D. Pusalkar observes, "A visitor to the ruins of Mohenjodaro is struck by the remarkable skill in town planning and sanitation displayed by the ancients, and as an English writer has observed, feels himself surrounded by ruins of some present-day working town in Lancashire."

Excavated ruins of Mohenjodaro, with the Great Bath in the front

Source: Wikipedia

Art and Crafts

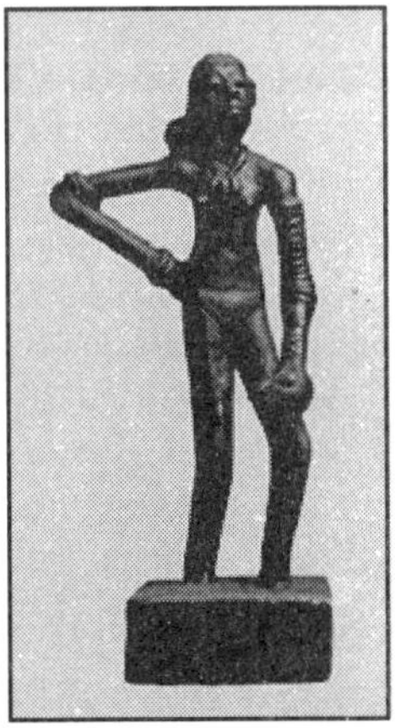

The "Dancing Girl of Mohenjodaro"

The attitude of the Indus valley people was utilitarian. Objects unearthed reveal that there was very little art for arts' sake in Indus valley. Their art of building proves it. There is no trace of ornamentation in houses and public buildings. Dr. A.L. Basham writes, "They were not on the whole an artistic people."

Yet the Indus people were not totally devoid of artistic talents. Their art specimens are found in pottery, figurines of males and females, seals and other small objects. All figurines are well baked and some of them are painted in red.

Animal figures are largely found in pottery. The most striking figurine is that of the bronze 'dancing girl' with her right arm on the hip and left arm hanging in a dancing pose. She is wearing a large number of bangles. The statue of the dancer is so beautifully executed that Dr. Tripathi remarks, "Its pose is so full of movement that there is hardly any parallel to it even among the sculptures of the historic period." The art of sculpture could also be seen in other statues, like that of a young bull, a strong watch dog, and a dancer standing on his right leg while raising his left leg in front. A well-known piece of art of the Harappan period is a stone sculpture of a bearded man discovered at Mohenjodaro. His eyes are half closed indicating a posture of meditation. Across the left shoulder is embroided shawl. All these statues faithfully display bodily features and look quite life like and realistic.

Statue of a Bearded Man, Mohenjodaro

Bead making and pottery making were other important crafts. Beads were made of precious and semi-precious stones such as agate and carnelian. Gold and silver beads have also been found. Potteries were chiefly wheel-made and were treated with a red coating and had decorations in black. These painted designs consist of horizontal lines of varied thickness. Birds, trees and animals are also depicted on these potteries.

The Indus people were also fully conversant with the art of carving. Their engravings on various seals are remarkable. These seals were mostly square in shape and were made of steatite. The seals depict different animals like bison, buffalo, tiger, deer, bull, and rhinoceros. However, there is no representation of horse on these. More than two thousand seals have been excavated from different sites so far.

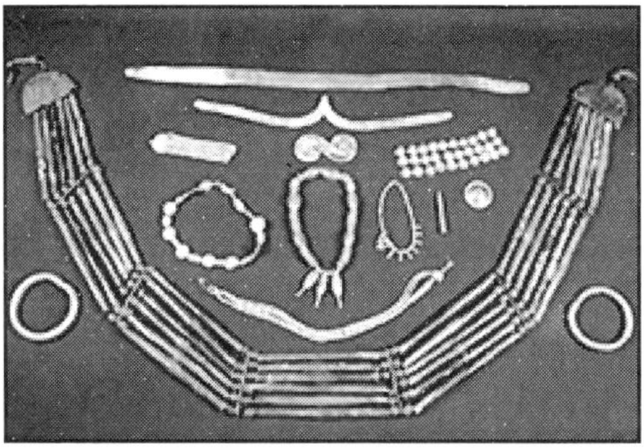

Bead jewellery

Religion

The religion of Indus people is known by the various seals, figurines and statuettes found at different sites. The Indus people mainly worshipped Shiva and Shakti (mother goddess). It is evident by the excavation of large number of female figurines. The terracotta figurines portray a standing and semi-nude female figure wearing a girdle or band round her loins, with elaborate head-dress and collar, etc. Some of the figures are smoke-stained and it is perhaps possible that some oil or incense was burnt before them. On a seal a male deity is also represented who is horned, three-headed, bearded and sitting in a yogic posture. He is surrounded by animal, viz. a rhinoceros, a buffalo, an elephant, a tiger and two deers. The deity is identified as Shiva and the presence of animals justify his title of 'Pashupati', the lord of beasts and animals and the yogic posture justifies his title of 'Maha-Yogi'. From the seals it appears that some sacrifices were made at the time of worship. Sir John Marshall discovered some polished and pierced stones on the basis of which he inferred that phallus worship was practiced by Indus people. Polished stones have been identified with linga and pierced stones with yoni. They were animist as they worshipped animals, trees, water, etc. They worshipped bull however horse was perhaps not known to them. The evidence of fire worship has also been found at some sites such as Kalibanga and Lothal. At Kalibanga, a series of raised brick platforms with pits containing ash and animal bones have been discovered. These are identified by many scholars as fire altars. There is no evidence of fire-pits at Harappa or Mohenjodaro. It also shows that the Harappans living in different areas followed different religious practices.

The so-called Shiva Pashupati seal

Mother Goddess Harappa

Economic Conditions

The main occupation of the Indus people was agriculture, spinning, weaving, and trade. The main crops grown were wheat, barley, sesasum, mustard, peas, millet and fruits. Earlier it was opined that rice was not known to them but now evidence of rice has been found at Rangpur and Lothal in the form of husks embedded in pottery. Cotton was another important crop. A piece of woven cloth has been found at Mohenjodaro. Although people were well acquainted with agriculture, we do not have any clear evidence of the tools used for agriculture. However, the furrows or plough-marks have been observed in a field at Kalibanga. All types of agricultural implements such as sickles, etc. have been discovered. Irrigation was also known to them. The animals were also domesticated for economic purposes.

Numerous spindles have been found at Mohenjodaro houses which show that the people in large numbers were engaged in spinning industry. From the discovery of many spindles and spinning wheels in the houses in the Indus valley, it is evident that spinning of cotton and wool was very common. Besides spinning and weaving, Indus valley people also practiced dyeing. All types of metal works including gold, silver, bronze, copper, tin, lead, etc. were practiced by them. Iron was unknown to them. They manufactured gold objects like beads, armlets, and other ornaments. But the use of silver was more common than gold. The people also manufactured knives, sickles, saws, axes, arrowheads, spearheads and razors of copper and bronze. It is important to note that the weapons of Harappan people were mostly defensive in nature. Stone tools were also commonly used. Copper was brought mainly from Khetri mines in Rajasthan. Gold could be obtained from Kolar fields in Karnataka and the river-beds of the Himalayan rivers. Silver must have come from Mesopotamia. Bronze was also used, though in a limited manner. The most important specimen of Bronze comes from Mohenjodaro in the form a figurine of 'dancing girl'.

But the most important industry of the Indus people was pottery. Many hand-made and wheel-made pots were used by them. The pots were burnt in kilns. These were treated with a red coating and had decorations in black. These were in various sizes and shapes. The painted pots were used for the presentation of valuables and the funeral urns. Brick industry too was flourishing industry. The Harappans manufactured seals of various kinds. More than two thousand seals have been discovered from different sites.

Mohenjodaro was not only a great industrial centre but also the great trading centre. It maintained both internal and external trade. It maintained trade relations with southern India, central India and north-western India. It also maintained trade relations with foreign countries like Mesopotamia. This has been proved by the discovery of Mohenjodaro objects at different sites of Mesopotamian and of Mesopotamian objects as Mohenjodaro. Mohenjodaro was thus economically prosperous due to flourishing trade and commerce. A large number of weights have been discovered from Mohenjodaro and Harappa. Ordinary pebbles were used as weights by the poor. Decimal system was known to them. Some weights are so small that they were perhaps used by the jewelers. A rod has been recovered which bears signs for measuring length. The seals were most probably used in connection with trade.

Seal of a humped-bull

Social Conditions

Since no written material about this civilization is available, therefore, the information has been collected on the basis of archaeological evidences. From the use of ornaments by the people, which have been found so far, it appears that whereas some persons used gold, silver and precious stone ornaments, the other satisfied themselves with inferior quality metal ornaments. This shows that the people of the civilization belonged to different social groups. The Harappan society was matriarchal in nature. This view is based on the popularity of the mother goddess as indicated by the finding of a large number of terracotta female figurines in Punjab and Sind region. The Harappan society comprised of various occupations including the priests, astrologers, physicians, traders, peasants and artisans, etc. The structural remains at sites like Mohenjodaro and Lothal show that different types of buildings that were used as residence by different classes. The presence of a class of workmen is proved by workmen quarters near the granary at Harappa. Similarly, the workshops and houses meant for coppersmiths and bead makers have been discovered at Lothal.

Since the people lived in different types of houses, but even then no single-storey house has been found, it appears that though society was economically divided, yet on the whole the people appear to be well do. From the fact that the people knew the use of decimal system it can be concluded that they were educated.

The dead bodies were generally rested in north-south direction with their head towards north and the feet towards south. The deads were buried with a varying number of earthen pots. In some graves, the deads were buried along with goods such as bangles, beads, cooper mirrors, etc. This may indicate that the Harappans believed in life after death. There are over fifty-five burial sites in the Indus civilization. The principal sites are Harappa, Kalibangan, Rakhigarhi, Lothal, Rojdi, and Ropar. At Lothal, three joint or double burials with male and female bodies together were discovered. And it has been suggested that this is an indication of some form of 'suttee' (a later Hindu custom in which wives end their lives after the death of her husband). Evidence of symbolic burial comes from Kalibanga. In symbolic burial, the burial contains pots but no bones or skeleton. In general, the burials in the Harappan period were all in brick or stone lined rectangular or oval pits. These different practices in different regions of Harappan civilization may reflect diversity in religious beliefs.

It has already been said that Mohenjodaro was cosmopolitan. It was the meeting ground of the people from different parts of Asia. The Indus valley people were both vegetarian and non-vegetarian. Wheat, barley, rice and milk must have been the important items of food. They also used fruits and vegetables. Their favourite fruit was date. They took fish, beef, mutton poultry, turtle and tortoise. The Indus valley people domesticated buffalo, sheep, goat, camel, cow and humped bull. They were also acquainted with some wild animals like lion, rhinoceros, tiger, monkey, bear, etc. Nothing was said about horse. Mongoose, squirrel, parrot, peacock, cat, etc. were also known to them.

The finds undoubtedly reveal a luxurious urban civilization. Men wore robes which left one shoulder bare. Women wore short or long skirts. The upper garment of a bearded statuette in steatite contains trefoil design. Most probably both cotton and woollen clothes were used by them. The clothes were also sewn as has been indicated by the discovery of needles and the statues. Needles were made of shell and ivory.

The Indus valley people were quite fashionable too. Shaving was known to them. Some were grew beards and trimmed them. They kept long hair. Various objects of head dressing have been found such as ivory combs, bronze mirror and razors for shaving, etc.

Both sexes, women more than men adorned themselves with a variety of ornaments like fillets, necklaces girdles, ear-rings, anklets and bracelets made of gold, silver, copper, shell and coloured stones like jade and lapislazuli. The naked bronze figurine of a girl, which has been called a "dancing girl" or a "temple dancer" has one arm fully covered with bangles from below shoulder to wrist. Almost all figures and carvings of women and goddesses show an elaborate coiffure arranged with the help of combs and hair-pins. Collyrium was used to beautify the eyes.

Dicing and some kind of chess were the pastimes of the elders while the children had play things like marbles, whistles and animals made of terracotta. The people were also fond of hunting. Indications are also there that birds are kept for fighting. Fishing was a regular occupation and game of theirs. Above all they were great lovers of music and dancing.

Many weapons have been unearthed from the Indus valley. The use of iron was not known to them. Their chief weapons were the axe, spear, bow, etc. Mackay says that the "Indus valley people were peace loving and unwarlike." Various household articles have been unearthed at Mohenjodaro. These are made of stone, shell, ivory, metal, etc. The most famous domestic articles were cake moulds, dippers, beakers, bowels, dishes, gobies, basins, pans, saucers, heaters, etc. Needles, axes, saws, sickles, knives, fish hooks, chisels, etc. have also been discovered. Some medicines were known to them. Coral and leaves of neem tree have been discovered. They all possess medicinal qualities.

Script

The Harappans were literate people. Harappan seals are engraved with various signs or characters. Studies suggest that the Harappan script consists of 270 distinct symbols and it was written from right to left. These are evidently pictographic in origin, which had an ideographic or syllabic character. Some signs have also been found on small tablets, ceramic pots and over a dozen other materials. However, the script has not been deciphered as yet. It is believed that they used ideograms, i.e. a graphic symbol or character to convey the idea directly.

While the Indus valley civilization is generally characterized as a literate society on the evidence of these inscriptions, this description has been challenged by few scholars, who argue that the Indus system did not encode language, but was instead similar to a variety of non-linguistic sign systems used extensively in the Stone Age. Others have claimed on occasion that the symbols were exclusively used for economic transactions, but this claim leaves unexplained the appearance of Indus symbols on many ritual objects, many of which were mass-produced in moulds. No parallels to these mass-produced inscriptions are known in any other early ancient civilizations. We do not know the language they spoke, though scholars believe that they spoke "Brahui", a dialect used by Baluchi people in Pakistan today.

Decline

The Harappan civilization flourished till 1900 B.C. After this the urban civilization started declining. This period is also known as Late Harappan Phase (1900-1400 B.C.). This phase was characterized by a gradual disappearance of the major urban traits such as town planning, trade, uniformity in weights and measures, etc. It was also marked by shrinkage of settlement area. The population appears to have shifted to other areas. It is not easy to say as to what specific causes led to the decay and disappearance of the Indus civilization. Different scholars have given different views as regard to its decline. Some of the main causes are as follows:

1. It is feared that certain wild and aggressive tribes from outside might have been attracted by the wealth and prosperity of the people and attacked the valley. The repeated attacks must have given a serious setback to the old civilization.
2. It is also possible that some serious earthquake might have rocked the cities and destroyed them.
3. One of the possibilities thought of is that the river Indus on whose valley this civilization developed might have changed its course thus forcing the people to desert the place.
4. Other causes considered responsible for the disappearance of the Indus civilization include either shortage of rainfall or destruction by flood or some other natural upheaval or natural calamities.

Thus, there is no single cause that can explain the decline of the civilization in totality. At the maximum these can explain the decay of certain sites or areas only. Hence, each theory has met with criticism. Nevertheless, the archaeological evidence indicates that the Harappan civilization did not collapse all of a sudden but declined gradually.

Chalcolithic Cultures

By the second millennium B.C. several regional cultures sprang up in different parts of the Indian subcontinent. These were non-urban, non-Harappan and were characterized by the use of stone and copper tools. Hence, these cultures are termed as Chalcolithic culture which means the stone-copper phase. The Chalcolithic people occasionally used low-grade bronze. They were primarily rural communities spread over a wide area in those parts of the country where hilly land and rivers were available. However, these were marked with basic uniformity in various aspects such as their mud structures, farming and hunting activities, etc. Wheel made fine pottery is the speciality of the Chalcolithic culture, though hand-made pottery is also present. The pottery of these cultures included black and red ware (BRW) and has been found in the shape of various kinds of bowls, basins, and spouted jars. They are all characterized by painted ceramic, usually black or red, a specialized blade and flake chalcedony and chert, and copper and bronze tools, though on a restricted scale. Their economy was based on subsistence agriculture, stock-raising and hunting and fishing. Some important non-Harappan Chalcolithic cultures are Banas or Ahar culture in southeast Rajasthan; Kayatha culture in Madhya Pradesh; Malwa Culture in western Madhya Pradesh; Jorwe culture near Pune in Maharashtra.

Residence

Though the Chalcolithic people of Harappa made extensive use of bricks, the Chalcolithic people in the rest of India did not use any such material. The walls were constructed out of mud or mud and wattle. The houses were either circular or rectangular on plan. The houses usually had only one room, but multi-roomed houses also existed as evident at Inamgaon. The houses used to be plastered with cow dung and lime.

Subsistence Pattern

The Chalcolithic people subsisted on farming and hunting-fishing. They reared cattle, sheep, goat, buffalo and pig, which were also slaughtered for food. A variety of crops were grown. The principal cereal was barley, though wheat was also cultivated. Rice is reported from Inamgaon. Other crops included bajra, jowar, millets, ragi, green pea, lentil, green gram, black gram, etc. Absence of dishes in Jorwe ware indicates that the preparations were semi-liquid. Neither plough nor hoe has been attested to at Chalcolithic sites, but perforated stone discs, which were used as weights for the digging sticks abound.

Fish and animal flesh formed an important part of the diet of the Chalcolithic people. Fish bones and fishhooks attest to active fishing. Hunting also was an important occupation for bones of wild animals like wild pig, deer, cheetah, etc. were found in the excavations. Cattle, buffalo, goat, sheep, pig and rarely horse were among the domesticated animals.

IMPORTANT QUESTIONS

1. Analyse the town-planning, social life and religious beliefs and practices of the Harappan people.
2. Examine the various views on the origin and decline of the Harappan civilization.
3. Discuss the economic activities of the Indus people.
4. Write a short note on the important buildings constructed by Indus valley people.
5. Discuss the settlement and subsistence pattern of the non-Harappan Chalcolithic cultures of India.

REFERENCES

Bashan, A.L., *The Wonder That Was India*, Delhi: Surjeet Publications, 2007.

Bhandarkar, D.R., *Some Aspects of Ancient Indian Culture.*

Chaurasia, R.S., *History of Ancient India Earliest Times to 1200 A.D.*, New Delhi: Atlantic Publishers, 2008.

Jayapalan, N., *History of India Upto 1206 A.D.*, New Delhi: Atlantic Publishers, 2001.

Majumdar, R.C. (Dr.), *An Advanced History of India*, New Delhi: Macmillan Publishers, 1978.

Vedic Age

5

Introduction

The next important age in the history of India after the Indus valley civilization is the Vedic Age. It was during this period that India presented to human culture one of its invaluable contributions—The Vedic Literature. It was attributed to the Aryans who flourished in India as a well-knit agricultural society. The period from 1500-600 B.C. has been referred to Vedic Age. It is so-called as the Vedas were composed during this period. This phase has been divided into Early Vedic Age (1500-1000 B.C.) and the Late Vedic Age (1000-600 B.C.).

Vedic Texts

The term 'Veda' has been derived from the Sanskrit word 'ved' which means 'to know' and 'veda' means 'knowledge'. The vast literature of the Aryans is generally divided into two parts. The first being 'shruti' or hearing, that which were directly heard by the sages from God, it included the four vedas, the Brahmanas, the Aranyakas and the Upanishads, etc. And the second being 'smriti' or remembering, which was composed by Rishis simply on the basis of their memory. It includes in its fold Vedangas, the Puranas, the Epics, etc. All these works were not composed at one time but at different times.

There are four Vedas composed during this whole Vedic Age. The four Vedas are Rig Veda; Sam Veda; Yajur Veda; and Atharva Veda. The Rig Veda was composed during the early Vedic Age so it reflects one stage of social and cultural development whereas the other three vedas reflect another stage. The rest of the three Vedas were composed during the later Vedic Age, i.e. during 1000-600 B.C. The later Vedic Age is also known as the 'Heroic Age' as the composition of two great epics, i.e. *Mahabharata* and *Ramayana* were also started during this period. Recently, the Rig Veda has been included in the list of literature signifying World Human Heritage.

Vedas are a collection of hymns, prayers, charms, and sacrificial formulae. The earliest work is *Rig Veda* which is a collection of 1017 hymns supplemented by 11 others called 'Valakhilyas'. It is arranged into 10 mandalas or books. These hymns were addressed to various Gods to bestow favours on the worshippers.

The *Sam Veda* contains 1540 'Richayen' or verses mostly taken from the Rig Veda but arranged in a poetic manner to facilitate singing. These are sung at the time of performing Yajanas. According to Dr. R.C. Majumdar, "While the Sam Veda is very important for the history of Indian music and throws interesting light on the growth of sacrificial ceremonies, its value as a literary work is practically nil".

The *Yajur Veda* is found in two recensions: Shukla (white) and Krishna (black). It is a collection of sacrificial formulae and the details of performing Yajanas. It is both in prose and poetry. It also gives the functions of Purohits. It has 40 chapters and about 2000 mantras.

The *Atharv Veda* is the fourth important Veda. It contains 20 mandalas, 731 Richayen and 5839 mantras. It is a collection of magical formulae and charms to ward off the evil spirits and diseases. It is partly in prose and partly in poetry.

Origin

The civilization of India after the Indus civilization is known to us through the Rig Veda. It is the first literary source for the history of ancient India. The authors of these Vedas were the Aryans. But who were the Aryans? Some scholars attaching more importance to the contents of the Rig Veda, maintains that the Aryans were of Indo European race. According to A.C. Dass, an Indian historian, the original home of Aryans was the Saptasindhu or the Punjab. Later Shri L.D. Kalla and Shri D.S. Trivedi also accepted this view. Some other scholars hold the view that the Aryans came to India from Central Asia. This theory is mainly associated with Prof. Max Muller of Germany. The late Bal Gangadhar Tilak was of the opinion that the original home of the Aryans was the Arctic region. In his book *Satyarth Prakash* Swami Dayanand Saraswati maintains that the Aryans were the inhabitants of Tibet. However, the most acceptable theory is of Central Asia. The supporters of Central Asian theory argue that: (a) A majority of eminent scholars support this theory; (b) The discovery of some inscriptions in Asia Minor prove that *Indra* and the *Varuna* Aryan gods used to be worshipped there in ancient times; (c) The animals, birds, trees and many agricultural products mentioned in Rig Veda were all found in Central Asia; and (d) Central Asia then was a fertile land which fulfilled all the needs of the Aryans.

Spread of Aryans in India

The Early Vedic Aryans lived in the area known as *sapta-sindhu* meaning area of seven rivers. This area largely covers the north-western part of south Asia up to river Yamuna. The seven rivers included Sindhu, Vitasta (Jhelum), Saraswati, Asikni (Chenab), Vipash (Beas), Shutudri (Sutlej), and Parushni (Ravi). In this area, the Rigvedic people lived, fought battles, grazed their herds of cattle and other domesticated animals. Gradually moving eastward, they came to occupy eastern U.P. (Kosala) and north Bihar (Videha) during the later Vedic period. Here they came in contact with the people who spoke languages different from their own and were living in this area for long. V.A. Smith holds that the Aryans migrated to India in about 1200 B.C. as Rig Veda was written between 1200-800 B.C. Dr. R.K. Mukerji held that the Aryans were occupying India in about 2500 B.C. They came to this country not all at once but they migrated in smaller groups over a longer period. As the fresh group came, it pushed the former inhabitants still deeper eastward in the country.

EARLY VEDIC PERIOD

Social Conditions

In early vedic times, family was the basic unit of life. Family was part of a larger grouping called clan. All the members of a clan were related to each other by blood relation. More than one clan formed the tribe or 'jana'. The Rigvedic society was patriarchal in nature and father wielded considerable authority over the children and other members of the family. The ties of marriages were held highly sacred and indissoluble. Monogamy was the usual norm but at times polygamy could be seen in upper classes. Though polyandry was known, it was not practiced. Woman was held in high respect and was given considerable freedom in choosing her husband. She was married long after they attained puberty. They often participated in philosophical debates like men with men. She could also take part in the proceedings of the tribal assemblies called *sabha* and *samiti*. Society being patriarchal, people usually prayed for sons. The birth of daughters was not desired, but once born they were treated with love and affection.

The early Aryans were simple people and the society was largely 'egalitarian'. But it refers to the division of society on the principle of the division of labour, i.e. the Brahmans, the Kshatriyas, the Vaishyas, and the Sudras. Although most scholars hold the view that caste system based on hereditary was absent in early vedic society. One's occupation decided its caste and one can easily change its caste by change of occupation. Members of a family could adopt different occupations. The following reference from Rig Veda also indicates the non-existence of rigid caste system during this period: "I am a poet, my father is a physician, my mother grinds corn on stone. Being engaged in different occupations we seek wealth and happiness, as crows seek food in different pastures. May thy bounties flow for our happiness, O' God." This shows the divisions in society were not sharp and rigid. However, certain differences did exist during the period. Varna or colour was the basis of initial differentiation between the Vedic and non-Vedic people. The Vedic people were fair whereas the non-Vedic indigenous people were dark in complexion and spoke a different language. Thus, the Rigveda mentions *arya varna* and *dasa varna*. Here, *dasa* has been used in the sense of a group different from the Rig Veda people.

The Rigvedic Aryans lived in villages. Houses were probably built of wood or reed. The members of a family lived in the same house. The master of the house was called *grihapati* or *dampati*. Their main food items were wheat and barley. Milk and its products like butter, ghee, curd, etc. were the chief diet. They also took fruits and vegetables. On certain religious occasions, *soma* (an intoxicating drink) was also taken. The meat of sheep and goat was freely eaten and even offered to gods. Their clothes were made of cotton, wool, or deer skins. Special attention was paid to dress and ornaments. Garments were often embroidered with gold. The use of gold ornaments was common particularly on festive occasions.

The Rigvedic people practiced various activities to amuse themselves. The main among them were racing, hunting, dancing, music, and boxing. The chariot-race was extremely popular and people practiced hunting of birds, lions, elephants, buffalo, deer and the wild boar. Women loved to display their skill in dancing and singing. The other important pastime was dicing, which frequently brought considerable loss to the gamester.

Economic Conditions

The Rigvedic people were mainly pastoralists, although agriculture was known to them. Cattle rearing were their primary occupation. They domesticated various animals like goat, sheep, cow, horse, etc. for milk, agricultural and other purposes. Herds of cattle were daily led to the pasture by the *gopa* (cowherd). However, the most respected was cow. A number of words are derived from the word 'go' meaning cow. A wealthy person was known as *gomat* and the daughter was called *duhitri* which means one who milks the cow. The cows were thought of provider of everything. Prayers were offered for increase in the number of cattle. Agriculture was also another important activity of early vedic people. Cultivated fields were known as urvara or kshetra. They produced yava or dhana, which was rather a generic word for cereals.

Though mainly pastoral and agricultural people, the early Vedic people were not indifferent to trade and industry. Commerce was largely in the hands of people styled as *Pani*. The main articles of trade were clothes, quilt and skins. Few people were also engaged in other economic activities like carpentry, weaving, chariot making, metal smeltary, etc. The carpenter not only made chariots, wagons, houses and boats, but showed his skill in carved work of a finer type such as artistic cups. The merchants organized themselves into guilds to protect their interests. The barter system was in vogue. The standard unit of value was the cow, but gold was also served as a means of exchange. The chief means of transport by land were chariots and wagons, run by horses and the oxen respectively. It is still a great controversy whether Rigvedic people knew marine navigation or not.

Religious Conditions

The Rigvedic Aryans worshipped nature. The early Vedic gods were generally personification of different aspects of natural forces such as rains, storms, sun, etc. The prayers including yajnas and sacrifices were offered to placate gods for physical protection and material gains. Sacrifice consisted of offering of milk, ghee, grain, flesh and soma. These sacrifices were organized by the chiefs of the tribes and performed by priests. Gods thus invoked in the sacrifices supposedly rewarded the sacrificers with success in wars, children, long life, and increase in cattle. The chief deities were *Agni* (fire god), the first hymn in the Rigveda addressed to him; *Indra* (god of war and rain war), most frequently mentioned god in the Rigveda; *Surya* (sun god), the most sacred hymn in the Rigveda known as the *Gayatri* is addressed to the rising sun; *Varuna* (god of moral code), looked after the affairs of empire and to whom people turned for forgiveness; *Vayu* (wind god); and *Pushan* (god of roads, cattle and herdsmen).

It is noteworthy that during the entire Vedic age neither temples were constructed nor people practiced image worship. These features of Indian worship emerged much later. Another important characteristic of Vedic Mythology is the domination of the male element. Goddesses like *Prithivi*, *Aditi*, *Usha*, and *Saraswati* occupy a very subordinate position. In this respect, the Vedic civilization presents a contrast to the prehistoric culture of the Indus valley, where the Mother Goddess was equal with her male counterpart.

Still another chief feature of the Vedic religion is the tendency towards monotheism. The hymns foretell the doctrine of universal unity, and express the belief that 'God is One', although he bears many names.

Political Conditions

The Rigvedic Aryans lived in tribes or 'Janas'. The chief of this unit was the political leader called *rajan* or chief. The main function of the *rajan* was to protect the *jana* and cattle from the enemies. The post of *rajan* was often hereditary, though at times, it was elected by tribe. Many officials assisted the king during this period. The chief among them were: *Purohita*, *Senani* and the *Gramani*. There is no official mentioned as a collector of taxes. The chief received voluntary offerings from people called *bali*. The *rajan* also dispensed justice. He was helped in his task by the tribal assemblies called *sabha*, *samiti*, and *parishad*. All aspects of life were discussed in these assemblies. These assemblies functioned more or less on democratic lines. But their decision was not binding on the king. The *sabha* was a small institution which dealt with the local problems and the *samiti* discussed national problems. According to K.P. Jayaswal, "The *Samiti* was the national assembly of the whole people, while the *sabha* was probably a standing and stationary body of selected men." Even women were also allowed to participate in the deliberations of the *sabha* and *samiti*. According to Prof. Ludwig, "The *samiti* was a more comprehensive conference including not only all the common people but also Brahmans and the rich patrons."

LATER VEDIC PERIOD

Social Conditions

There came a bitter change in the society. The family remains the basic unit of the later Vedic society. The caste system became rigid. Many sub-castes were born causing complexities of the caste system. The institution of *gotra* developed in this period. This means that people having common *gotra* descended from a common ancestor and no marriage between the members of the same *gotra* could take place. Polygamy became frequent, though people preferred monogamy. The position of women degraded in the society.

Some restrictions were imposed on the women. She could not freely participate in public meetings. The birth of a son was preferred than of a daughter, who in a text has been mentioned as source of all sorrows. Women, dice and wine were considered as three great evils. The priestly class became more dominant with the increase in the importance of religious rituals and sacrifices. Along with the *Brahamans*, the *Kshatriyas* controlled all major aspects of the society. However, the centre of gravity was king and not the priest. The *Vaishyas* were more in number and were engaged in agriculture, trade and other artisanal activities. They paid gifts and taxes to the above two varna, i.e. the Brahamans and the Ksahtriyas. The fourth varna was of *Shudra* who were at the bottom and did all menial works. They were not entitled to the ritual of *upanayana samskara* (sacred ceremony to acquire education). It was just the beginning of the imposition of many other disabilities on the shudra. From *Manusmriti* we get to know about the different stages of life or ashrama system. They are *brahmacharya* (student life), *grihastha* (householder), *vanaprastha* (hermitage) and *sanyasa* (mendicant). Each period consists of 25 years. Little change can be traced in the way of house-building and style of dress. However, the eating of meat was being looked upon with disfavour.

Economic Conditions

The chief occupation of later Aryans was agriculture. There was some improvement in the methods of cultivation of the people. There is mention of use of six and eight oxen in ploughing. The God Indra came to be associated with the 'lord of plough'. The number and varieties of plant food increased. People now cultivated wheat, rice, sugarcane, millet, etc. The beginning of the use of iron during 1000 B.C. led to further expansion of the Aryans. Mention has been made that the early Aryans knew of a metal called *ayas* which was either copper or bronze. And the later Aryans knew of *shyama* or *krishna* meaning black to denote iron. As the north-eastern part of India, where the later Aryans moved is covered with dense forest it could not be cleared with copper tools. From the excavations near *doab* area a large number of Painted Grey Ware (PGW) has been found which indicates the expansion of the economy.

The variety of industrial occupations was remarkable. Specialization had gone far. The maker of the bows was parted from the maker of the bow-strings and of arrows, the chariot-maker from the carpenter. Women too participated in industrial life as makers of embroidered dress workers. The settled life due to improvement in culture led to the emergence of many cities like Videha, Kausambhi, Kosi, Ayodhya, Hastinapur and Indraprastha, etc. came into prominence and were great centres of trade and industry.

Religious Conditions

Religious beliefs underwent a great change. In this period, the great gods of the Rigvedic period like Indra, Varuna and Surya, etc. receded in the background and new gods like Vishnu, Shiva, Rama and Krishna had came into picture. The religious ceremonies had become very complex and complicated which cannot be performed by common people themselves. The sacrifices and yajnas became very elaborate and very expensive lasting for months. Some of the important yajnas were—*ashvamedha*, *vajapeya*, *rajasuya*, etc. They had to be performed in the presence of many priests. The Brahmanas in return got lots of gifts in the form of *dana-dakshina*. A lot of sacrifices of animals destroyed the cattle wealth and hampered the economy. The common people developed faith in magic, spirits and witchcrafts. They also had faith in transmigration of soul.

Political Conditions

Monarchy was the form of government during the later Vedic period. The king became very powerful and now all his officers thought it appropriate to please him. There were elaborate coronation rituals to establish the supremacy of the chiefs. The territorial idea gained ground. They spread from Punjab to Gangetic plain. They even penetrated south up to Godavari. Regular elementary armies were maintained. The popular democratic assemblies gradually declined as office of chief became hereditary. The people lost control over their *rajan*. Kingdoms became large in size and were ruled over by powerful kings. Administration by now had become very complicated. There were many administrative officers who were appointed by the king. They also became very powerful. There was deterioration in their moral character as they indulged in liqour and luxury. The army and other officers were paid by the taxes collected from the common people in the form of *bali*, the *shulka*, and the *bhaga*.

CASTE SYSTEM

Meaning of Caste System

A caste may be defined as a group of families internally united by peculiar rules for the observance of ceremonial purity, especially in the matter of diet and marriage. It is a kind of social exclusiveness in the matter of diet and marriage. Caste systems are the 'frame' of society. Each of its limits had its particular duties and privileges. According to Manu, the Brahman was to study and teach, perform yajana and assist others in doing it. In return of his service, he received gift. The second caste in order of importance was Kshatriyas. The Kshatriyas had to minister and protect people. They performed yajanas and fought bravely in the battlefield. The people of the third caste were called 'Vaisyas'. They tended cattle, performed yajanas, etc. and carried on trade and agriculture. The people of the fourth caste were the Sudras who did menial service and ministered to the physical comforts of the community.

The law books also refer to mixed castes which originated from intermarriages and illicit relations. Next there were the non-Aryans the Mlechchas, Chanslars and Swapakas who were considered even lower than the Sudras. Originally, the Aryans were divided into four 'Varnas' which with the lapse of time began to be known as four main castes of the Hindus. At first the caste of a man was determined on the basis of his ability and occupation he adopted. He could easily change his caste with the change of his occupation. But later on birth and not the worth became the basis of caste. This system assumed such a rigidity that it became quite impossible for anyone to change one's caste. During the course of time, these four castes were further divided into numerous sub-castes and at present we find the Hindu society divided into more than 3000 castes and sub-castes. The *Manusmriti* mentions four varnas. It makes distinction between varna and caste. The four varnas or orders were with reference to the occupations of men:

1. The learned, literate and priestly order or the Brahmans;
2. The fighting and governing classes the Rajanyas or Kshatriyas;
3. The trading and agricultural people or Vaisyas; and
4. Common, humble folk-day labourers and menial workers whose business was to serve their betters. They were called Sudras.

It is difficult to say when the caste system took its origin. First of all there were two divisions—white complexioned Aryans and secondly the dark coloured non-Aryans or Dasyus. The very word varna indicates colour. Thus, the caste system was originally on the basis of varna or colour. The Aryans considered themselves superior to the coloured races of India. Some historians believe that the caste divisions were on the basis of division of labour.

Growth of Caste System and Its Basic Causes

The basic causes of growth of the caste system in India are the following:

1. Vastness of the Country: Gradually, the Aryans spread throughout the country and they had to adjust themselves in matters of food, living and occupations according to the nature and climate of the place. As today we being one of the same family, people are divided into Gujaratis, Punjabis, Marwaris, Madrasis, Kashmiris, etc.

2. Inter-caste Marriage: Some Aryans, disregarding the customs of their castes got married to women of other castes. The descendants of such couples got to be regarded of new and different castes.

3. Supremacy of the Brahmans: The Brahmans in order to maintain their supremacy laid a great stress on the principle that caste depended upon heredity and not on occupation. Their selfishness hardened the rigidity of the caste system.

4. Rise of Buddhism and Jainism: On account of simplicity of the new religions, Buddhism and Jainism, many Hindus were attracted towards the new religion. But when Buddhism declined these people formed their own castes.

5. Adoption of Different Crafts and Specialisation: When some persons of a caste achieved skill and perfection in any particular craft and art, they began to impart that knowledge to the members of their own families alone and excluded others from that art. Gradually, they began to marry within their particular group and assumed the form of various sub-castes, e.g. Sunar, Lohar, Carpenters, Weavers and Oilmen, etc.

6. Influence of Islam: The process of the Muhammadan conquest tended to lighten the bonds of caste. The Hindus defended themselves passively by the increased rigidity of caste association.

7. Effect of the Decline of Ahimsa in Caste System: The Jains and Buddhists preached the doctrine of Ahimsa. It gave rise to many new castes. Those who did not like taking meat left their own folds and formed their new castes.

8. Foreign Element in the Hindu Religion: Many foreign tribes came to India from time to time. The Sakas, Huns, the Greeks, etc. embraced Hinduism and formed separate castes of their own. In this way, the number of castes and sub-castes went on increasing in India and now on place of four original castes or varnas there are over 3000 castes.

Merits of Caste System

Caste system has rendered some useful source to the Hindu society. Some of the chief merits of the caste system are the following:

1. Purity of Blood: Each caste made rigid rules as regards marriage and inter-castes marriages were strictly forbidden. It resulted in the preservation of purity of blood.

2. Protection of Hindu Civilization and Culture: The Aryans were able to protect their culture on account of their caste. It was their rigid caste system that did not allow them to marry non-Aryan women. The foreigners who came to India during the course of time could not conquer the Aryans culturally. They strictly kept aloof in food and matrimonial relations.

3. Social and Economic Security: The caste system provided social security to its members. The people of one caste cooperated and helped one another. Caste system survived as it possessed economic security. Son inherited profession of father.

4. Specialisation in Various Occupations: The caste system helped greatly in specialisation of arts and crafts. They attained perfection in particular occupation. They imparted knowledge of that art only to the members of their own tribes.

5. Social Control: Each caste has its own rules and regulations which bind the members of a particular caste. If anybody dares to break the rules, he is thrown out of the caste. This fear of social boycott exercised social control over the members of a caste.

6. It has Absorbed Foreigners in Hindu Fold: Those foreigners who settled down in India once for all, were absorbed in Hindu fold. In course of time they forgot that they once came to India as invaders. Examples of such conversion are Kanishka and Minindra, etc.

7. Advancement of Art and Literature: Caste system helped a great deal in the advancement of art and literature. Each caste has its own specific occupation and the members specialised to carry on the art to the perfection. They did not reveal the trade secrets of their knowledge to any outsider. The art secrets were kept limited to the members of the castes only.

8. The State had not to Spend Separately on Education and on Military Training: The task assigned to the Brahman class was that of teaching. They imparted knowledge to the proper persons without charging any fee.

9. The Caste System Checked Establishment of Military Dictatorship: The caste system helped in the decentralization of power. The Brahmans possessed spiritual power, the Kshatriyas has physical power and Vaishyas wealth and Shudras service powers, so there was no fear of military dictatorship.

Demerits of Caste System

The caste system did probably more wrong than good. It proved very harmful to the Hindu society. It proved harmful in the following ways:

1. It was the Cause of Mutual Jealousy: With the increase in rigidity of the caste system, the whole society was soon divided into hostile groups with sharp differences. It proved a stumbling block in the way of unity. The people could not unite even against the foreign invaders. Caste system proved anti-national and disasterous to the Hindu society.

2. It Proved a Hinderance on Personal Advancement: The caste system became rigid and hereditary and it became growingly difficult for a member of one particular caste to adopt any other profession of his own choice. It led to the stagnation of individual talents and merits.

3. It Checked Inter-caste Marriages: The caste system proved a great hurdle in the way of inter-caste marriages narrowing down the circle of marriages.

4. Main Cause of Untouchability: It gave rise to the cursed untouchability. The upper classes began to regard themselves far superior to the sudras and illiterated them. The status of equality was denied to man.

5. A Check on Religious Advancement: The people of each caste began to consider themselves superior to others. They did not mix freely and discussed problems. This social aloofness proved very detrimental to the advancement of religious thought and philosophy, etc.

6. Anti-democratic: A caste ridden society can never be democratic. In the absence of equal status law and political rights are denied to a larger section of society.

7. Responsible for Narrow Outlook: Caste system does not allow people to mix freely and exchange ideas. The Indians disliked to go to foreign countries. They had remained a stay at home people. It makes people narrow-minded.

8. Anti-feeling of Universal Brotherhood: Caste system is against the feeling and spirit of universal brotherhood. The institution of caste exclusiveness has outlived its utility and may be discarded; the sooner it is done, the better it is. Lord Mahavira, Buddha, Lingyat and social reformers like Swami Dayanand, Mahatma Gandhi, Nanak and Kabir have all condemned caste system. Practice of untouchability is a blot on the fair frame of Hindu society. It is why the new constitution of free India has banned it altogether, but caste system is still alive and important in India.

IMPORTANT QUESTIONS

1. Examine the controversies on the advent of the Aryans and discuss the key features of the political, social and economic conditions of Northern India from 1500-1000 B.C.
2. How far do you think iron tools were responsible for surplus production and socio-economic changes during the later Vedic period?
3. Discuss the emergence of caste system in later Vedic period. Also discuss its merits and demerits.
4. Outline the important features of society as depicted in the early Dharmashastras.
5. Point out the differences and similarities between the Vedic and the Indus valley people.

REFERENCES

Basham, A.L., *The Wonder That Was India*, Delhi: Surjeet Publications, 2007.

Chaurasia, R.S., *History of Ancient India (Earliest times to 1200 A.D.)*, New Delhi: Atlantic Publishers, 2008.

Jayapalan, N., *History of India (up to 1206 A.D.)*, New Delhi: Atlantic Publishers, 2001.

Majumdar, R.C., *An Advanced History of India*, New Delhi: Macmillan Publishers, 1978.

Sharma, L.P., *History of Ancient India (Pre-historic Age to 1200 A.D.)*, New Delhi: Konark Publishers, 1996.

Religious Ferment in Sixth Century B.C.

6

Introduction

The sixth century B.C. was an age of extraordinary mental and spiritual unrest. Increase in agriculture and trade increased social inequality and conflict. People wanted some kind of relief from the present social problems like hatred, inequality, violence, cruelty and falsehood. The prevalent Brahmanical system or religion was very complicated and attached with itself more importance to sacrifices and rituals. Therefore, when new sects such as Jainism and Buddhism preached the gospel of peace, non-violence and social equality people welcomed them. These new social orders were free from unnecessary and expensive sacrifices and rituals. A number of teachers went to different parts of the country to propagate the new philosophy of life and death.

The arrogance of the Brahmans and the class pride arouse apprehension in the minds of other classes. These classes rebelled against the monopoly enjoyed by the Brahmanas in regard to the exclusive possession of superior knowledge of Shastras. As the Shastras were written in Sanskrit which was not understood by the common people, the Brahmanas interpreted the religion according to their convenience. Hence, less privileged were eagerly looking for some better and easier path to attain salvation in life. Besides, the general economic progress had increased the prosperity of the vaishyas and their proportion in the society was more than any other class, they wanted a better social position. Therefore, they preferred to patronize non-Vedic religions like Buddhism and Jainism through substantial donations.

JAINISM

Origin

Earlier it was thought that Lord Mahavira was the founder of Jainism. But this notion has been proved wrong by Jain traditions. According to these traditions, Jainism is as old as the Rigvedic civilization. The religious priests of the Jains were known as Tirthankara. The first Tirthankara of the Jains was Rishabha. Lord Mahavira was the last of the twenty-four Tirthankaras. We do not have much information about the first twenty-two Tirthankaras. But have some information about the 23rd Tirthankara, i.e. Parasavnath. It is said that he was opposed to polytheism and performing of expensive yajanas. He was also opposed to animal sacrifice. He laid emphasis on Ahimsa, truthfulness and non-attachment. Parasavnath is believed to have lived a hundred years and died only 250 years before his more celebrated successor, Lord Mahavira.

Life of Lord Mahavira (599-527 B.C.)

Lord Mahavira was born in about 599 B.C. in a village near Vaishali in Bihar. He was the twenty-fourth and the last Tirthankara of Jainism. His original name was Vardhamana. His parents were Siddhartha, a wealthy noble man and Trisala sister of Chetak, an eminent Lichchvi prince of Vaisali. Vardhamana married Yasoda and had a daughter by her. Mahavira renounced the worldly life at the age of 30 and became an ascetic. It is said that in his long journey to attain enlightenment he never changed his clothes and completely abandoned them when he attained kevalam (supreme knowledge) in the 13th year of his penance. He is also known as Arhat (great) and Jina (conqueror). Any soul that has conquered its own inner enemies and achieved the state of supreme being is called a jina. For 12 years he lived on alms and wandered from place to place. He reduced himself to skeleton. Lord Mahavira is said to have fasted to death in about 527 B.C. at Pava (near modern Patna). He used Prakrit, the language of the masses to propagate his teachings. He had about 14000 disciples.

About two centuries after Mahavira's death the Jain church got divided into two sects: Digambaras "sky clad" who remain naked and Svetambaras "white clad" who wear white clothes.

Main Doctrines

Jainism encourages spiritual development through cultivation of one's own personal wisdom and reliance on self-control through vows. The Mahavrata or Great Vows of Jainism are: Ahimsa (non-violence); Satya (truthfulness); Asteya (non-stealing); Aparigraha (non-possession or non-materialism); and Brahmacharya (celibacy). It is advocated that the first four vows were preached by Parasvnath and the last vow, i.e. celibacy was added by Mahavira. Jainism believed in extreme form of Ahimsa. As per them every living being has a soul. Hence, no harm or ill-treatment be done to any living being. Jainism believe that the main goal of human life is the purification of soul and attainment of nirvana, which means freedom from the cycle of birth and rebirth. And this could be achieved by following the Triratne or three jewels. They are Samyak Darshana (right view); Samyak Gyana (right knowledge); and Samyak Charitra (right conduct). Right conduct means observance of the five vows. The most distinguishing feature of Jainism was the concept of anekantavada or syadavada. It means that the truth can be viewed from aneka or various angels.

Jainism does not believe in the existence of God. It believed that man is the architect of his own destiny. They do not believe in the creation of universe by God. As per V.A. Smith, "The belief in the supreme deity, the creator of the universe is emphatically denied. God is defined as being only the highest, the noblest and the fullest manifestation of all powers which lie latent in the soul of man." Another important feature of Jainism was its emphasis on extreme form of penance, austerity, and strict non-violence. Death by gradual starvation was recommended. It is only through hard life and self-sacrifice that a person becomes virtuous and great. According to Lord Mahavira, our actions or deeds influence our soul; these good or bad deeds do not come to an end here but also pass on to the next life. Therefore, one should always do good deeds or Karmas. As it is not easy to abstain from worldly pleasure, Mahavira prescribed few austerities such as fasting, gradual abstention from food, from a full meal to one morsel, begging, giving up delicious food, of mortification of the flesh, etc.

Contribution of Jainism

Jainism had its effect and deep influence on social, political and religious life of the people. It gave a serious setback to caste system. It freed religion from sacrifices and yajnas. Lokmanya Tilak credited Jainism with influencing Hinduism and thus leading to the cessation of animal sacrifice in Vedic rituals. Bal Gangadhar Tilak has described Jainism as the originator of Ahimsa. Jains encourage their monks to do research and obtain higher education. Thus, Jain monks and nuns, particularly in Rajasthan, have published numerous research monographs. This is unique among Indian religious groups and parallels Christian clergy. Jain libraries are the oldest in the country. Jains built many beautiful temples and thus contributed to architecture. Anga, Upanga and Mula sutra are beautiful literary pieces and are of great historical significance and importance.

Decline of Jainism

In the beginning, it received much support but gradually it began to disappear. Some of the causes responsible for its decline are as follows:

1. It was not a missionary religion. Lord Mahavira himself preferred silence over its propagation and did not propagate it like Buddha.
2. It was a type of extremist religion involving extreme type of sacrifices and strict discipline which common people could ill-afford.
3. In actual practice some of the principles like ahimsa could not be followed.
4. It could not receive the same amount of royal patronage as enjoyed by Buddhism.

Due to the above said reasons, it could not attract the masses in large number.

BUDDHISM

Origin

The founder of Buddhism was Gautama Buddha or Siddhartha, who was born in 566 B.C. at Lumbini garden near Kapilavastu in Nepal. He belonged to a Kshatriya clan. His father, Suddhodana was the chief of the Sakya clan. His mother, Maya died seven days after giving birth to him. Therefore, he was brought up by his stepmother Prajapati Gautami. He was married to Yashodara at an early age and had a son named Rahula. From his early childhood, Gautama showed inclination towards philosophy. He discussed serious problems of life pertaining to life, death, soul and God, etc. Hence, his marriage could not influence his mind for long. As the tradition describes it, he was greatly moved at the sight of an old man, a sick person and a dead body, and then attracted by the appearance of an ascetic (sanyasin), he left his home, wife, and small son and the luxurious life at the age of 29 years. He kept on wandering for about seven years and then attained knowledge at the age of 35 at Bodhgaya under a peepal tree. He practiced continuous meditation and got enlightenment. Henceforth, he was begun to be called Buddha or the enlightened one. He delivered his first sermon at Sarnath near Varanasi in northern India. This event is known as dharma-chakra-pravartana (turning of wheel of law). His first converts were five bhiksus. They together with the Buddha formed the first Sangha, the company of Buddhist monks, and hence, the first formation of Triple Gem, viz. Buddha, Dharma, and the Sangha was completed. For the next 45 years he travelled to distant places to preach people in their own language. He travelled to Kosala, Magadha, Vaishali, Kausambhi and Anga. Buddha passed at the age of 80 years in about 486 B.C. at Kusinagar (in modern Deoria district of U.P.). He is considered as one of the greatest saints like Christ who influenced mankind.

Doctrines of Buddhism

The original Buddhist texts were written in Pali and are collectively known as *Tripitaka* (three baskets). According to *Tripitaka*, the four noble truths or arya satya was the first teaching of Gautama Buddha after attaining Nirvana. At Sarnath, Buddha preached that the four noble truths are: (i) world is full of sorrows (dukkha); (ii) every sorrow has a cause (dukkha samudya), sorrows are the outcome of endless desires; (iii) sorrows could be extinguished (dukkha nirodha); and (iv) the remedy to avoid these suffering is Eight-Fold Path. In order to end our sorrows, Buddha recommended the Eight-Fold Path, these are:

(i) Right view—Understanding the truth of life and viewing reality as it is and not as it appears.

(ii) Right resolution—Intention of renunciation, freedom and harmlessness.

(iii) Right speech—A person should always speak the truth and also politely to others to avoid conflicts.

(iv) Right conduct—A person should not engage in inhuman activities like theft, murder, etc. and should always work for the welfare of the society.

(v) Right living—One should not earn his livelihood from wrong practices such as selling liquor, slaughtering animals, etc.

(vi) Right effort—One should keep only good thoughts in mind and avoid evil thoughts.

(vii) Right mindedness—A person should always be aware of evil thoughts and deeds and should never allow them to enter his mind.

(viii) Right concentration—One should meditate with complete concentration.

Lord Buddha completely emphasized on good character and morality and stressed that one should follow ahimsa in thought, speech and also in action. There should be no injury to living beings and there should be no animal sacrifice at all. Though Buddha preached that the ultimate aim of one's life is to attain Nirvana, which is attainment of knowledge and Moksha, he was silent about God as for him God had no hand in the attainment of Nirvana. Buddha asked his followers to avoid the two extremes, of indulgence in worldly pleasure and the practice of strict abstinence and asceticism. This philosophy of *madhyama marga* or the Middle Path is reflected in all the issues related to Buddhism. He laid stress on truth, charity, purity and control over passions. As per him every person is the arbiter of his own destiny. Good deeds lead one to higher life while evil deeds retard the progress. Buddha organized the *sangha* to spread his doctrines. He allowed lower varna people and women to join the *sangha* thus challenging the superiority of Brahmanism. Four Buddhist Councils were responsible for the compilation of Buddhist scriptures called Tripitikas—first at Rajgriha, called by Ajatashatru; second called by Kalaasoka at Vaisali; third at Patliputra during the reign of Ashoka; and the fourth under Kanishka at Kashmir. In the fourth council during the reign of Kanishka, Buddhism split into two major sects called Hinayana and Mahayana. Mahayana adopted Sanskrit as its language and started worshipping Buddha in the form of an idol, while Hinayana continued to follow Pali and treated Buddha as a guide.

Causes of Spread of Buddhism

The sixth century B.C. was a period of complicated rituals and sacrifices. The common people could hardly understand the reason for costly yajnas. At this time was born a simple yet influential man, Lord Buddha. He was an ideal man. He was embodiment of truth and non-violence. He practiced what he taught. He was a symbol of piousness. Therefore, Buddhism spread throughout India very quickly. Even during the lifetime of Lord Buddha his philosophy had been accepted by lot of people. The major reasons for the spread of Buddhism are as follows:

1. Buddha propagated his message in Pali, as it was easily understood by the people.
2. Buddhism did not believe in any caste system and so it opened its door for all races.
3. Buddhist councils were organized from time to time to review their own work as well as removing the doubts of people.

4. Monks and nuns were sent to different parts of the world to spread the message of Buddha to far areas also.
5. Buddhism got patrons in the form of great kings like Asoka, Kanishka and Harsha. They made Buddhism their state religion. It was due to Asoka's effort that Buddhism spread to Sri Lanka.
6. The new religion appealed to reason and applied logic to everything.

Buddhism came at a time when the people had grown sick of complicated rituals, sacrifice and yajanas. They were tired and confused of costly religion. They readily accepted the new philosophy of Buddhism which was free from such complications.

Buddhist Councils

From time to time Buddhist councils were held to solve problems concerning Buddhism.

First Council

It was held in about 483 B.C. at Rajgriha (Magadha) soon after the death of Lord Buddha. It was presided over by Mahabharta and attended by 500 Buddhist scholars including Ananda and Upali. It collected and gave definite shape to teachings of Buddha which are contained in three Tripitakas. The council was held under the patronage of the ruler of Magadh Ajatashatru. Vinaya Pitaka lays down the rules of the Sangha, Sutta Pitaka deals with the slaves and legends regarding the life of Gautama Buddha and Abbhidamma Pitaka deals with the religious philosophy of Buddhism.

Second Council

It was called by Kalaasoka in about 387 B.C. at Vaishali. About 700 Bhikshus took part in this council. It considered relaxation of monastic discipline and also introduced some changes in the old scriptures. Some Bhikshus who disregarded the strict rules of the Sangh organisation were turned out of the order. They organised their own organisation 'Mahasanghik'.

Third Council

Third council was held in about 251 B.C. at Patliputra during the reign of Ashoka. It was presided over by Muggaliputta and aimed at reforming monastic life. It also aimed at strengthening the teachings and practices of Buddhism. The proceedings of the council continued for over a month and about 1000 Bhikshus took part in the deliberation. After this council missionaries were sent out to foreign countries to spread the message of Buddhism.

Fourth Council

It was held in about 100 A.D. during the reign of Kanishka. The council met at Kundalvana in Kashmir. It was presided over by Vasumittra. The aim of the council was to bridge the differences which had crept in Buddhism. Ultimately, Buddhism got divided into Hinayana and Mahayana schools of thought. The council prepared commentaries on scriptures of Buddhism and decided to send missionaries to propagate Buddhism.

Split in Buddhism

During the lifetime of Gautama Buddha, Buddhism made rapid progress. The people gladly accepted the new faith. But the situation radically changed after the death of the master. There was no able successor of Lord Buddha who could keep Buddhism under his control, with the result that the differences erupted in the new faith. For some time efforts were made to narrow down these differences. But during Kanishka's reign at the time of the Fourth Council these differences became unbridgeable and Buddhism got divided into two main schools of thought to Mahayana and Hinayana. The basic differences between the two branches of schools are the following:

(i) Idol Worship: The Mahayana school of thought believed in the worship of Buddha and treated him as God. They made his beautiful idols in different forms and shapes. The followers of Hinayana school disliked idol worship. They did not regard Buddha as God but was of the view that he was a great man with pious soul and pure ideas. Buddha should be respected not as God but an embodiment of goodness and purity.

(ii) Faith and Reason: The followers of the Mahayana school laid stress on faith rather than on reason while the followers of Hinayana faith laid stress on reason than on faith.

(iii) **Language:** The religious language of the Mahayana school of thought was Sanskrit while the followers of the Hinayana school of thought regarded Pali as their religious language.

(iv) **Rituals:** The Mahayanas followed many religious rituals and laid stress on idol worship and prayer of Buddha. But the followers of the Hinayana philosophy did not believe in rituals, nor had they any faith either in worship or the prayer. On the other hand, they stressed on purity of heart, simplicity and self-control.

(v) **Aim of Life:** For the followers of Mahayana school of thought, the ultimate aim of life was not to get 'Nirvana' or to get rid from the cycle of birth and rituals. But the followers of the Hinayana school did not believe that going to heaven should be the aim of a man's life but they believed that Nirvana or salvation should be the aim of a man's life in this world.

Buddhist Literature and Art

The Buddhist literature contained in *Jatakas* and *Tripitakas* has great importance in all spheres of life in Indian history. The *Jatakas* deal with the birth stories of Buddha in his previous lives. From the study of the *Jatakas*, we come to know how Buddha was against the caste system. *Jatakas* throw light on the important events of Kasi, Kosala and Magadha states besides the popular superstitions and customs of the people during the period 600-400 B.C. Other important Buddhist literature books are *Vinayapitaka*, *Milindapanho*, *Dipavamsa* and *Mahavamsa*. Buddhism became an inspiration for the promotion of art and architecture, in the form of stupas, rock-cut caves and paintings. These can be noticed at Sanchi, Barhut, Amravati, Ajanta, etc. Buddhism inspired Gandhara and Mathura schools of art.

Decline of Buddhism

Buddhism very rapidly found its root in India and was also welcomed abroad. But this popularity did not last long and after some time this new religion also saw decline. Following are the main causes for the decline of Buddhism:

(i) **Reform in Hindu Religion:** The people left Brahmanism and accepted Buddhism not because they had lost faith in the basic principles of Brahmanism but because they condemned outward rituals and ceremonies. When the Brahmanas openly saw revolt against them they reformed their shortcomings with the result that the people came back to their fold again.

(ii) Withdrawal of Royal Support: Under Asoka, Harsha and Kanishka, Buddhism received royal support with the result that the people openly followed Buddhism under royal patronage. But after the death of Harsha, Buddhism lost royal patronage which gave it a serious setback. Sungas, Kanvas and Gupta rulers supported Hinduism.

(iii) Division among Buddhists: As long as the Buddhist stood united they were not challenged. But when they were divided into Mahayana and Hinayana schools of thought, Buddhism was weakened. Cultural criticism lowered its prestige in the eyes of other people and made it unpopular.

(iv) Opponent Sects: After some time Vaishnavism and Saivism came to the front and they made the path of Buddhism difficult. No longer it was smooth sailing for the spread of Buddhism.

(v) Lack of Influential Personality: Buddhism failed to produce any influential personality after the death of Buddha, which could catch the imagination of the masses. On the other hand, Brahmanism produced Kumarul Bhatt and Shankaracharya, etc. who could refute Buddhist philosophy.

Similarity between Buddhism and Hinduism

Lord Buddha did not intend to make Buddhism a new religion. What he intended was that the Hindu religion should be reformed. He simply desired to end the evils which crept in old Hinduism. Buddhism took from Hinduism the theories of rebirth and karma. Both the systems resemble each other in their general character of the spirit of toleration. The main points of agreement between the two great religions are as under:

(i) Nirvana Theory: Both Buddhism and Hinduism agree that the aim of human life is the attainment of 'Nirvana' by leading a good and moral life.

(ii) **Karma Theory:** In both the religions, it is believed that people get the reward or punishment according to their own actions. Not even angels can exempt men from the consequences of their deeds.

(iii) **Emphasis on Morality:** In both the religions, great emphasis is laid on leading a good and moral life. A man's real worth can be judged only by the virtuous life he leads. Thus, both of them resemble in this respect.

(iv) **Toleration:** The Hindus have never exerted pressure on others for increasing their number. In the same way, Buddhists believe in full cooperation and complete tolerance. Thus, religious tolerance is the anchor sheet of both the religions.

(v) **No Faith in Idol Worship in the Beginning:** In the beginning, the Aryans did not practise idol worship but later on they began to worship various gods and goddesses and began to worship their idols. Similarly, Gautama Buddha did not sanction the image worship but after his death his followers began to make his statues and worship him. Thus, in both the religions, idol worship became a common feature.

Differences between Buddhism and Hinduism

Buddha did not intend to found any new religion different from Hinduism but with the lapse of time certain differences appeared between Buddhism and Hinduism. They differ with each other in the following areas:

(i) **Different Views about Vedas and Sanskrit:** Buddha did not accept Vedas as divine books nor does he admit Sanskrit as a superior language while the Hindus regard Vedas as the divine knowledge. Their knowledge is considered necessary for the salvation of man. In the same way, Sanskrit language is regarded as a sacred language.

(ii) **Hinsa and Yajanas:** Buddha has opposed *hinsa* and *yajanas* as absolutely fruitless. It is main actions which make or mar his future. Our past actions have fashioned our present life and our present deeds will fashion our future when we are reborn. Man must relish the fruits of the true he had grown for himself. How can sacrifices, yajanas help a man to get rid from his past deeds? The Hindus regarded yajanas essential for getting salvation.

(iii) **Caste System:** The caste system is an important feature of Hinduism. The Buddhists have no faith in class distinctions and caste hatredness. For them all are born equal and nobody can claim superiority on the basis of his birth. Deeds count, not caste.

(iv) **Presence of God:** The Hindus believe in the presence of all powerful (omnipotent) God who is the creator of this universe. But Buddha was silent over the question of his presence. God has no hand in the attainment of Nirvana while the Hindus attach great importance to God and many deities.

(v) **Buddhist Sangha:** Unlike Hinduism, Buddhism was a missionary faith and every attempt was made by the Bhikshus to propagate and preach this religion in India as well as in far off lands. The Buddhist Sanghas were highly organised of the Bhikshus where all the work was systematically planned and implemented. The propagation machinery was highly specialised. The Bhikshus were men of high character and learning. They created a good influence over the people who flucked to their fold in large numbers. The Brahmanism made no attempt to propagate their religion in foreign countries, so Buddhism became popular in foreign countries.

(vi) **Status of the Brahman:** The Purohits and Brahmans occupied highest status in society and no religious act and yajana was considered to be complete without their help. In contrast to this, Buddhism regards all people equal and no special importance was given to them. Buddhism does not accept Brahmans and Purohits helpful in the attainment of 'Moksha' or salvation.

(vii) **Knowledge and Action:** Hinduism laid stress on knowledge while Buddhism emphasized action.

Buddhism as a Reform Religion

To begin with Buddha did not wish to make Buddhism a new religion. He simply wanted to reform the existing Hindu religion and remove the evils that had crept in it during the course of time. He condemned sacrifices, costly *yajanas*, rites, etc. He also condemned the caste system which was disintegrating the Hindu society. Basically, he believed in the theory of karma and Nirvana. In the true spirit of the Vedas, he laid stress on purification of mind and soul rather than on outward appearance. He did not condemn any fundamental principle of the Hindu religion. He revolted against the animal sacrifices. The common people had already tired of them. He did not acknowledge the sanctity of the Sanskrit language only because it was beyond the common people. It was not the spoken language of the masses. He condemned the caste system because the common man had already been tired of it and seen its fatality. In fact, the main principles on which Buddha laid emphasis were taken from the Upnishads of the Hindus. The theory of Ahimsa, protest against ritualism and sacrifices, challenge to the superiority of the Brahmans merely on the basis of birth. Condemnation of class distinctions which Buddha preached was not new. All these were already in the air and in the mind of the people. They were already hinted in the Upnishads.

It can be said in conclusion that Buddhism was not a new religion but just a reform movement within Hinduism. According to Dr. V.A. Smith, "Buddha may be justly regarded as having been originally a Hindu reformer. He did not give any holy scripture to his disciples nor did he condemn any fundamental principles of Brahmanism. He himself was a Kshatriya prince and was inspired by the Upnishads. He only gave his teachings in the common language of the people."

AJIVIKAS

Buddhism and Jainism were not the only religions, which challenged brahmanical dominance. According to the Buddhist sources, more than 62 sects and philosophies flourished in this period. One of these sects was known as Ajivika, which was founded by Makkhali Goshal, a friend of Mahavira, the 24th Tirthankara of Jainism. His doctrines and those of his followers are known only from Buddhist and Jain sources, which state that he was of humble birth and died shortly before the death of Buddhism. Mauryan kings donated several caves in the honour of Ajivika monks. They were under a rigorous discipline similar to that of the Jains, which involved complete nudity.

Ajivikas believed that transmigration of the human soul was determined by a precise and non-personal cosmic principle called *niyati*, destiny or fate and was completely independent of the person's actions. They are believed to be strict fatalists, who did not believe in karma or the possibility of free will.

The Ajivikas appear to have attained some importance in the time of Asoka as the latter mentions them side by side with the Buddhists and Nirgranthas and he instructed his Mahamatras to look after their welfare. He even gifted two caves in the Barbara hills to the Ajivikas. However, they could not establish any tradition like other religious beliefs. They had no scriptures. They only retained some local importance in a small region of eastern Mysore and the adjacent parts of Madras, where it survived until the 14th century, after which we hear no more of it.

IMPORTANT QUESTIONS

1. Describe the causes leading to the rise of new religious sects in the 6th century B.C.
2. Analyse the chief doctrines of Jainism and Buddhism and account for their popularity.
3. Account for the factors responsible for the decline of Buddhism in India.
4. What are the similarities and differences between Hinduism and Buddhism?
5. Write a short note on:
   (a) Buddhist Councils.
   (b) Ajivika sect.
   (c) Difference between Hinayana and Mahayana sects of Buddhism.

REFERENCES

Chaurasia, R.S., *History of Ancient India (Earliest times to 1200 A.D.)*, New Delhi: Atlantic Publishers, 2008.

Jayapalan, N., *History of India (up to 1206 A.D.)*, New Delhi: Atlantic Publishers, 2001.

Majumdar, R.C., *An Advanced History of India*, New Delhi: Macmillan Publishers, 1978.

National Institute of Open Learning, *E notes.*

Sharma, L.P., *History of Ancient India (Pre-historic Age to 1200 A.D.)*, New Delhi: Konark Publishers, 1996.

Mahajanapadas

7

Introduction

The 6th century B.C. was not only a period of socio-religious development but it also witnessed the political development in the form of rise of *sixteen mahajanapadas*. We know that the later Vedic people started agriculture in the Ganga basin and settled down in permanent villages. In this period, the centre of economic and political activity shifted from Haryana and western UP to eastern UP and Bihar, which received more rainfall hence, was more fertile. As now the iron ore reserves were near it became easier to clear the thick vegetation with iron tools, which in turn brought more area under cultivation. This increase in agriculture and settled life led to the rise of *Mahajanapadas* in north India in 6th century B.C. A ploughshare dated to *c.* 500 B.C. has been found from Jakhera in Etah district in western UP, which clearly indicates the growth of agriculture.

After the decline of Harappan civilization the urban life also declined. And during the Vedic period the people lived village life. The urban life again emerged during the 6th century B.C. in the form of *sixteen mahajanapadas*. Hence, this era is also known as period of *second urbanization*. However, the urban centres now emerged in Ganga basin instead of Indus plain. Many janapadas when conquered by one king together formed the Mahajanapada, which literally means *great kingdoms*. Most of them were located north of Vindhyas, between Bihar in the east and north-west frontier of the subcontinent.

S.No.	Mahajanapadas	Capital	Modern Location
1.	Kasi	Varanasi	Banaras
2.	Kosala	Sravasti	Eastern U.P.
3.	Vajji	Vaishali	Vaishali
4.	Malla	Kusinara	Deoria, U.P.
5.	Chedi	Suktimati	Bundelkhand
6.	Vatsa	Kausambi	Allahabad
7.	Kuru	Indraprastha	Meerut and S.E. Haryana
8.	Panchala	Kampilya	Western U.P.
9.	Matsya	Viratanagara	Jaipur
10.	Surasena	Mathura	Mathura
11.	Avanti	Ujjaini	Madhya Pradesh and Malwa
12.	Gandhara	Takshasila/Taxila	Rawalpindi
13.	Kamboja	Rajapura	Rajori and Hajra (Kashmir)
14.	Asmaka	Potana or Potali	Bank of Godavari
15.	Magadha	Girivraja	Gaya and Patna
16.	Anga	Champa	Munger and Bhagalpur

The historians have constructed the political history of India from 650 B.C. to 325 B.C. on the basis of Brahmanical, Buddhist and Jain works. Hence, it can be said that firstly most of these states were monarchical in nature and the republican form of government came later. This view has been supported by K.P. Jayaswal and Romila Thapar. According to Romila, "The more independent Aryans rebelled against monarchial rule and established republics which were more in keeping with tribal traditions." Most of kingdoms were always in conflict with one another. During the lifetime of Gautam Buddha, all the above states were reduced to only four important states. These are Vatsa, Avanti, Magadha and Kosala. These four kingdoms gradually absorbed the other neighbouring small and weak kingdoms. The political fight among these *mahajanapadas* led ultimately to one of them, namely Magadha to emerge as the most powerful state and the centre of a vast empire.

HARYANKA DYNASTY

Bimbisara

The first monarch about whom anything substantial is known is Bimbisara, or Srenika, of Haryanka dynasty. According to Buddhist chronicles, Bimbisara ruled for 52 years roughly from 544 B.C. to 492 B.C. He pursued a three-edged policy to expand his empire. These are: matrimonial alliances; friendship with strong rulers; and conquest of small and weak kingdoms. The annexation of Anga was the first step taken by Bimbisara in order to extend his empire. He annexed the kingdom of Anga with its capital at Champa, by defeating its ruler, Brahmadatta and incorporated Anga into Magadha. Hence, he is regarded as the real founder of the Magadhan imperial power. Under the policy of matrimonial alliances, he married Kosaladevi the princess of Kosala and the sister of Prasenjit. This lady brought with her the territory of Kasi as dowry. Bimbisara's other wives were Chellana, daughter of Lichchhavi chief at Vaishali and daughter of the chief of Madra clan in Punjab. Ajatashatru was the son of Lichchhavi princess. He was a contemporary of both Buddha and Mahavira and paid equal respect to them. Tradition says that in his old age the king was murdered by his son Ajatsatru, who was very eager to capture the throne. Some Jain texts tell us that Bimbisara himself took poison and died. Even according to V.A. Smith, "The young Ajatashatru was impatient to grab the throne and accused him of having done his father to death by the agonies of starvation."

Ajatashatru

Next in the succession was Ajatashatru or Kunika, as Jains call him. He ruled from 492 B.C. to 460 B.C. He was an aggressive and powerful person. In the lifetime of his father Bimbisara, he was given the viceroyalty of Champa. Like his father Ajatashatru also believed in the expansion of his empire by military conquest. He first came in conflict with his maternal uncle Prasenajit over the territory of Kasi, which was given to her mother in dowry. It was only after a fierce battle that Kasi remained with Magadha. Rajagriha was the capital of Magadha and was naturally fortified by five hills. But Ajatashatru in order to repel the Vrijis had built a fort at Pataligrama, on the bank of the Ganges. After 16 long years of war Ajatashatru succeeded in breaking the might of Vaishali. Therefore, he not only retained Kasi, but also added Vaishali to Magadha. Kosala was humbled but not crushed. Both Mahavira and Buddha are said to have died early in his reign. Ajatashatru is said to have paid a visit to Buddha and expressed deep remorse for his sins. He professed his faith in Buddha and completely dedicated himself to Buddhism. It was under his reign that the first Buddhist council was held at Rajagriha. He also suffered a fate similar to his father and was assassinated by his son Udayin. Ajatashatru was succeeded by five kings who were not worthy of kinghood.

Successors of Ajatashatru

According to the Buddhist and Jain texts, the successors of Ajatashatru ruled one after another for about 116 years. Most of these rulers were mere names and not much is known about them. However, the immediate successor was Udayin. He is credited with the foundation of the city of Pataliputra. The history of Magadha after Udayi is obscure. The names of the rulers vary in Buddhist and Puranic traditions. Finally, a popular rising took place and drove the last descendant of Bimbisara from the throne. A minister named Shishunaga was placed on the throne. It was after his name that the dynasty is named Shishunaga. The most important achievement of Shishunaga was to defeat Avanti (Malwa) and make it a part of Magadh. The successor of Shishunaga was his son Kalashoka. It was during his reign that the second Buddhist council was held. The last ruler of the line was murdered about the beginning of the 4th century B.C. by Mahapadma Nanda, the founder of the Nanda dynasty.

NANDA DYNASTY

Nanda dynasty ruled Magadha, in north India from *c.* 343 to 322 B.C. Indigenous sources, both Brahmanical and Jaina, suggest that Mahapadma Nanda was the founder of the Nanda dynasty and he belonged to a low caste or at least a non-kshatriya caste. He brought many neighbouring kingdoms under his rule. It is stated that the Nanda dynasty retained its throne for two generations only, Mahapadma and his eight sons. Dhanananda, the last of this list was, a powerful contemporary of Alexander the Great. The Nanda line ended with him in about 322 B.C. when Chandragupta laid the foundation for Mauryan power. He possessed a large army and added Kalinga to his empire. He is believed to be an arrogant and oppressive ruler, hence most hated among his subjects. He imposed heavy taxes on the common man. It is mentioned by Chandragupta that the reason why he could overthrow the Nanda dynasty was the prevailing antipathy towards Dhanananda among his people.

Now the question arises as how Magadha could establish gradually its dominance over all other states of the period. Magadha certainly benefited from numerous able and ambitious rulers, but its strength is attributed greatly to geographical factors. Firstly, it is a fertile plain which provide a large amount of agriculture surplus; secondly its earlier capital Girivraja was surrounded by five hills, which helped it to provide natural fortification; thirdly the southern forests gave it timber and elephants easily; and fourthly the iron deposits were near to Magadha which made the Magadhan weapons far superior and agricultural tools more productive. These material advantages made Magadha to become more powerful than the other fifteen *mahajanpadas*.

IMPORTANT QUESTIONS

1. What do you understand by 'Second Urbanization'? Explain it in the context of socio-economic changes in the 6th century B.C.
2. What are the factors that helped Magadha emerge as the most powerful state amongst the *sixteen mahajanapadas*?
3. Write a note on the political condition of India in the 6th century B.C.

REFERENCES

Chaurasia, R.S., *History of Ancient India (Earliest times to 1200 A.D.)*, New Delhi: Atlantic Publishers, 2008.

E notes, National Institute of Open Learning.

Raychaudhuri, H.C., *An Advanced History of India*, New Delhi: Macmillan Publishers, 1978.

Sharma, L.P., *History of Ancient India (Pre-historic Age to 1200 A.D.)*, New Delhi: Konark Publishers, 1996.

Smith, Vincent A., *The Early History of India*, New Delhi: Atlantic Publishers, 1999.

Mauryan Empire

8

Introduction

The establishment of Mauryan dynasty by Chandragupta Maurya in 322 B.C. marks a turning point in the history of early India. The Nandas had definitely raised Magadha to the status of political pre-eminence in India and its boundaries were certainly extensive. Yet it was short-lived, misgoverned and had not reached the epitome of its power. The Mauryas achieved all, which the Nandas had failed to do. The Mauryas established a vast empire in India whose boundaries included not only the entire Indian territories (excluding the southern part) but also the territories beyond India in the north-west. This empire was not only extensive and stable but its rulers also provided sound administration for the welfare of their subjects.

Sources of Mauryan History

Mauryan dynasty is the first historical dynasty about which some definite historical material is available. In the words of Dr. Smith, "The advent of the Mauryan dynasty marks the passage from darkness to light." The following are some of the chief sources of the formation regarding the Mauryan dynasty:

(1) **Edicts:** The Asokan edicts are the most important source of information and there are at least 44 such edicts which have been found inscribed on rocks, caves and pillars. These are written in Brahmi script and Prakrit language. They enlighten us about the important aspects, of social life in those days.

(2) **Accounts of Foreign Writers:** Among the descriptions of foreigners, the most important account is of Greek writer Megasthenes. He was deputed by Seleucus Nector as an ambassador at the court of Chandragupta Maurya. He has

given detailed description about Chandragupta's administration and the society of that time. His writing *Indica* is not available now but all later foreign scholars of that age used it as the source material for their writings.

(3) **Kautilya's *Arthashastra*:** The *Arthashastra* of Kautilya or Chanakya is the most important secular account of the history of Mauryans. Chanakya was the Prime Minister and great supporter of Chandragupta. He helped Chandragupta in destroying the Nandas and capturing the throne of Magadha. *Arthashastra* is a treatise of not only economics but also of sociology, moral principles, polity, etc. Thus, it throws flood of light on the contemporary social, political and economic life of the country. It also gives wealth of information regarding duties of the king, his administration and welfare activities.

(4) ***Mudrarakshasha*:** It is a play written by Vishakhadutta in Sanskrit during 5th century B.C. He has given details about the fall of Nandas and the rise of Chandragupta to Magadha throne with the help of his teacher Kautilya.

(5) **Buddhist Texts:** Two Ceylonese Buddhist texts called *Dipavamsa* and *Mahavamsa* are the most useful texts. These were written in Pali language. These texts are very helpful in knowing about emperor Asoka and his son Kunal.

(6) **Jain Texts:** As compared to Brahmanic and Buddhist text, Jain texts throw more useful light on the early history of Mauryans. It throws more light on the history of Chandragupta Maurya. It declared that towards the end of his life Chandragupta had embraced Jainism.

(7) **Brahmanical Texts:** Among the Brahmanical texts, the *Puranas* are the most useful. They tell us about the social, political and cultural life of Mauryan period. But they cannot be relied completely as they are mixed up with many imaginary things also. So, the opinion of Brahmanic texts should be judged by comparing them with Jaina and Buddhist texts.

(8) **Archeological Sources:** The ruins of monuments of that age such as stupas, viharas and caves, remains of the palace of Asoka at Kumhara and the punch-marked coins are a great source for the reconstruction of the Mauryan history.

Chandragupta Maurya (322–297 B.C.)

The first historical paramount sovereign or Emperor in India, Chandragupta's accession to the throne may be dated with practical certainty in 322 B.C. Traditions differ regarding the antecedent of Chandragupta. According to one account, he was the son of the last Nanda from his Sudra concubine Mura by name from which was derived the name Maurya. The Greek writer, Justin says that he was a man of humble origin; Jain tradition regards Chandragupta as the son of daughter of the chief of a village of peacock breeders (Mayur Poshak). It is noteworthy that peacock figures as the emblem of the Mauryas in some punch-marked coins and sculptures, etc. Besides, the Buddhist text *Mahavamsa* described that Chandragupta belonged to a Kshatriya clan called Moriya.

Chandragupta probably held a high post in the Nanda army. But somehow some differences arose between him and his master and he had to run for his life towards Punjab. He then liberated the north-western part of India from Greek domination, grabbed power in Magadha from the hands of its tyrannical ruler Dhanananda, and established a mighty empire in India whose boundaries crossed the natural frontiers of India. He inherited a large army of the Nandas, which he increased until it numbered 30,000 cavalry, 9,000 elephants, 600,000 infantry, and multitude of chariots. He used it to conquer almost whole of north, the north-west, and a large part of the peninsular India.

Chandragupta founded the Mauryan Empire by overthrowing the Nanda dynasty. The adviser of this youthful and inexperienced Chandragupta in this revolution was a subtle Brahman named Chanakya, or Kautilya by whose aid he succeeded in seizing the vacant throne. Chanakya was an important minister in the court of the Nanda rulers. He was ill-treated by the Nanda king and he vowed to destroy their kingdom. He met the young Chandragupta in the Vindhya forest. As Chanakya was well versed in politics and the affairs of the state, he groomed Chandragupta and helped him raise and organize an army. Thus, with the help of Chanakya, Chandragupta overthrew the last Nanda ruler and became the king. Chanakya became the Prime Minister in the court of Chandragupta. But according to V.A. Smith, "the people did not gain much by the change of masters, because Chandragupta, after his victory, forfeited by his tyranny all title to the name of liberator, oppressing with servitude the very people whom he had emancipated from the foreign thraldom". He died in 297 B.C. after a reign of 24 years. As per Jain traditions Chandragupta abdicated his office during the last years of his life and accompanied Bhadrabahu, the recognized founder of one of Jainism's two principal sects, Digambara, to the south, lived as an ascetic at Sravana Belgola in Mysore, and ultimately committed suicide by gradual starvation at that place, where his name is still held in remembrance. V.A. Smith was of the impression that the tradition has a solid foundation on fact.

Conquests of Chandragupta

We do not have definite details about the extent of Chandragupta's empire. However, Junagarh Rock Inscription of Rudradaman proves the inclusion of Saurashtra. The Greek writers Justin and Plutouch also refer him as the master of the whole India. The Tamil writer Mamulanar alludes to the Mauryan invasion of the far south. Jain traditions testify to Chandragupta's connections with North Mysore. Thus, it appears that the conquest of a large part of India is to be ascribed to him. Recently discovered Kandhar Inscription of Asoka conclusively proves that the territory in question formed part of Asoka's empire. Asoka did not conquer the region but inherited it. It is believed that Chandragupta mostly passed his life in fighting battles. Bindusar, his son and Asoka's father is not known in history as a great conqurer, while Asoka conquered Kalinga only. It may reasonably be assumed that the empire over which Asoka ruled was mostly the creation of his grandfather Chandragupta. Thus, his empire was very vast. It extended from Bengal in the east to the Hindukush in the west and from the Himalayas in the north to the south of Vindhayas. Kabul, Herat, Kandhar, Baluchistan, Uttar Pradesh, Bihar, Bengal, Gujarat, Kathiawar were all included in his empire.

Administration under Chandragupta Maurya

Chandragupta Maurya was not only a conqueror but also a great administrator. The administrative machinery founded and organized by him worked well throughout the Mauryan period.

Civil Administration: The head of the government was the king himself. He was supreme and the final authority in all matters, military, judicial and executive. He received petitions from his subjects, granted audience to envoys and looked into the state finances. He was assisted by a 'Mantri-Parishad'. The *Arthashastra* mentions Amatyas, Mahmatyas, Adhyaksha, Purohit, Senapati, Yuvaraja, Antarvesika and Parasatri, etc.

Provincial Administration: The empire being vast it was divided into a number of provinces. The important provinces were governed by Kumaras or princes of royal blood. Taxila, Tosoli, Swarngeri (Songir) and Ujjain were such provinces. The system of espionage was perfect and prevented harassment of the common people. The monarch kept himself posted with the current affairs and events of his kingdom by the secret system of spies who supplied information.

Municipal Administration: The local affairs were under a commission of six board each consisting of five members incharge of different departments such as industry, art, medical aid, registration of deaths and births, trade and commerce, etc. The municipal commissioners were expected to manage the affairs of the city and to maintain temples and works of public utility.

Military Organisation: Chandragupta Maurya had a formidable force which was efficiently maintained by the war office consisting of 30 members divided into six boards of five each. The several departments assigned to them were admiralty, transport and commissariat, infantry, cavalry, chariots and elephants, etc.

Penal Code: Offenders were ordinarily punished with fines varying in amount but there were also terrible punishments. Injury to an artisan or evasion of tiles on sales led to the award of capital sentence and perjury was punishable with mutilation of the limbs. Kautilya prescribes death even for a petty theft by a government servant; judicial torture like whipping, etc. was authorized and openly used for extracting information from criminals and suspects. These rigorous punishments had gone a long way in the prevention of crime, so crimes were very few.

Sources of Income and Expenditure: Land revenue was the main source of income. The share of the crown was 1/6 of the gross produce but the proportion varied according to place and other circumstances. Dues from mines, forests, customs, tolls and ferry duties, fees, taxes and fines were other sources of revenue. The revenue thus collected by the 'Samaharta' was spent on maintenance of the king and his court, on the army, defenses of the kingdom, salaries of the officers, allowances, charities, religious provisions and works of public utility like roads, canals, building, etc.

Judicial System: The Mauryan rulers took interest in the administration of justice. Regular courts were established throughout the length and breadth of the empire. In the villages the cases were divided by the Panchayats. According to Megasthanese, Chandragupta sometimes sat for the whole day in hearing cases and giving 'decision'. The appeals from the lower courts could be made to the provincial courts and from provincial courts to the central court of Pataliputra. The laws were very severe. No leniency was shown to the offenders and criminals. Justice was impartial, fair and inexpensive and quick.

Spy System: The credit for the efficient running of the administration goes to the spy system of the Mauryas. The spies kept the king informed of everything going on in the kingdom as well as the neighbouring states. They also kept the king informed of the public opinion on various important matters. There were many women among those spies. They were highly dependable. Most formidable were Vish Kanyas.

Chandragupta ascended the throne at an early age and reigned only before he was fifty years of age. In this brief span of life he did much. The expulsion of the Macedonian garrisons from the Punjab, the decisive repulse of Seleukus the Conqueror, the subjugation of at least all northern India from sea to sea, the formation of a gigantic army, and the thorough organisation of the civil government of a vast empire were no mean achievement and fairly entitle him to rank among the greatest and most successful kings known to history.

Chanakya

Chanakya or Kautilya sometimes also called as Vishnugupta (flourished during 300 B.C.), is the greatest figure of wisdom and knowledge. He was born in a Brahmin family and received his education at Taxila. He was the adviser and prime minister of Chandragupta Maurya. He is best known for his work *Arthashastra* (science of artha or material gain), which is an ancient Indian treatise on statecraft, economic policy and military strategy. Even the German scholars have established beyond doubt the fact that it is the most authentic composition of Maurayan age. According to V.A. Smith, "This book is of extraordinary value and interest, shedding more light upon the realities of ancient India, especially as concerns administration, law, trade, war, and peace, than any text which we possess." This book was discovered by Shamashastri in 1905 A.D. who also translated and introduced this book to the public. Chanakya was a great force in the overthrowing of Nanda dynasty. It was he who encouraged and guided Chandragupta to dethrone Dhanananda, the tyrant ruler of Nanda dynasty. Hence, Chandragupta laid the foundation of the greatest dynasty in ancient India, The Maurayan Dynasty. Saptanga theory is given in *Arthashastra*, which includes for the first time the complete definition of seven organs of the states. The seven organs or elements are:

1. **Swami (king)**: *Swami* means the head or the master. According to Kautilya's view, the *swami* should be awarded with qualities flowing from a noble birth, wisdom, enthusiasm and personal ability.
2. **Amatya (minister)**: *Amatyas* constitute the second important element and consist of all high officers such as the chief priests, ministers, collectors, officers in charge of civil and criminal administration, officers in charge of harems and the superintendents of various departments.
3. **Janapada (country)**: The term *janapada* indicates both the territory and its population. As per Chanakya's

view, a territory should have good climate and it should yield grain with little labour. Further, it should be inhabited by industrious people.

4. **Durga (fortified city)**: Kautilya refers to the construction of the fortress for the protection of the empire people.
5. **Kosa (treasury)**: In the opinion of Chanakya, *kosa* or treasury is very important for keeping the army and other officers loyal. And it should be earned by legitimate sources.
6. **Danda (army)**: It means coercive power mainly in the form of army. According to Kautilya, this element consists of infantry, chariots, elephants, and cavalry.
7. **Mitra (ally)**: The seventh and the last element mentioned by Chanakya is *mitra*. According to him, an ally is one with whom there is no possibility of rupture and one who is ready to come for help anytime.

These seven elements despite being 'enumerated' separately stand in a closet possible relation to one another and are in themselves 'mutually serviceable'.

Bindusara (298-272 B.C.)

When Chandragupta either abdicated or died, in the year 298 B.C., he was succeeded by his son Bindusara. He is also known as Amitraghata, 'Slayer of foes'. The cordial relations between India and the Hellenistic powers, which had been initiated by Chandragupta and Seleukus, continued unperturbed throughout the reign of Bindusara, at whose court Megasthenes was replaced by Deimachos, as ambassador. Bindusara promoted trade and cultural interactions with Greeks, but not much is known about him. Nothing is recorded about the reign of Bindusara, nor is any inscription or monument of his time is known. However, according to the *Puranas* he ruled for a period of 25 years. The Ceylonese traditions say that his reign lasted for 27 or 28 years. Bindusara continued to follow the annexation and conquest policy of his father within the borders of India. The limits of the empire of Asoka, successor of Bindusara, are well known with sufficient accuracy. It is recorded that Asoka fought only one war of conquest, i.e.

Kalinga War. It is more probable that the conquest of the south was the work of Bindusara than that it was affected by his busy father. But according to V.A. Smith, "The ascertained outline of the career of Chandragupta is so wonderful, and implies his possession of such exceptional ability, that it is possible that the conquest of the south must be added to the list of his achievements." With the brief flash about the life Bindusara, father of Asoka, we will now move on the life and achievements of one of the greatest monarchs not only of India, but of the world.

Asoka (272-232 B.C.)

Early Life

Asoka Vardhana or Asoka, was born in 302 B.C. He succeeded to the throne in 272 B.C., although his coronation ceremony took place in 269 B.C. as his claim to the throne was disputed. Asoka served his apprenticeship as the governor of Taxila and Ujjain during the lifetime of Bindusara. According to the Buddhist tradition, he got possession of the throne by massacring his ninety-nine brothers. This seems however to be untrue and not worthy of belief. According to V.A. Smith, "These idle stories seem to have been invented by the monks chiefly in order to place a dark background of early wickedness behind the bright picture of his mature piety." Asoka was selected by his father as Crown Prince, out of his several brothers, on account of his ability and fitness for the imperial succession. Earlier, like his predecessors, he was also pleasure-loving. He was fond of hunting and went out for pleasure excursions. But he changed completely after the war of Kalinga and became one of the noblest kings known to history. According to Dr. Majumdar, "He is one of the most remarkable personalities in the history of India."

Kalinga War

The most important event of Asoka's reign was conquest of the kingdom of Kalinga, around 261 B.C. It is the strip of territory extending along the coast of the Bay of Bengal from the Mahanadi to the Godavari in which large number of people were killed or imprisoned. According to Dr. R.K. Mukherji,

"The horrors of war worked a revolution in his character." It was perhaps this bloodshed which filled his heart with remorse and he decided to abandon the policy of military expansion. This war proved a turning point in his career which produced results of far-reaching consequences. He declared that never again in future should ambition lead him to inflict such grievous wrongs upon his subjects. He announced that he would in future follow *dhammaghosha* (drum of *dhamma*) than *bherighosha* (war drum). The king then acted upon what he professed. Gradually, he came under the influence of Buddhist teaching. His devotion and commitment increased as more and more years rolled on. He begs his descendants to get rid of the notion that the prime duty of a king is to conquest by means of arms and war.

Asoka's *Dhamma*

Asoka in history is known for his policy of *Dhamma*. The word *dhamma* is the Prakrit version of the Sanskrit word *dharma*. He is praised not so much for his militaristic activity as for his policy of *dhamma*. Although in the beginning he was a great conqueror, yet after the war of Kalinga he made it the aim of his life to employ his unlimited autocratic power over a vast empire in the teaching, propagation, and enforcement of the ethical system, which he called the Law of Piety or Duty (*dhamma*). According to some scholars, Asoka was a follower of Buddhism and through *dhamma* he tried to propagate the teachings of Buddhism. But it does not seem to be true as *dhamma* is a moral code of conduct. *Dhamma* was not any fundamental principle of Buddhism alone but it was an essence of all the religions. It was a collection of some of the good principles of all the religions. It consisted of well-known principles of morality, i.e. compassion (*daya*), charity (*dana*), truthfulness, purity and gentleness. In the seventeenth and eighteenth years of his reign, he proclaimed the principles of his rule to his people in a series of edicts engraved upon the rocks, including Minor Rock Edict I and the Fourteen Rock Edicts. Nowhere in his edicts, remarks Dr. Tripathi, "does he mention the chief characteristics of Buddhism to wit, the Four Noble Truths, the Eight-fold Path and the goal of Nirvana". Asoka did not seek to impose his personal religion upon the people. He laid emphasis on obedience and respect for parents, teachers, preceptors and elders. A closer look at Asoka's edicts exemplifies that basic principles of Asoka's *dhamma* included:

(i) *Samyam* or mastery of senses—One should have complete control on his senses to avoid any unpleasant activities;

(ii) *Bhava-shuddhi* or purity of thought—Not to allow evil thoughts to come to mind or not to have ill-will for anyone;

(iii) *Kritajnata* or gratitude;

(iv) *Daya* or kindness;

(v) *Dana* or charity—According to Asoka, one should give education to the illiterate, money to the poor and the knowledge of *dharma* to everyone;

(vi) *Satya* or truthfulness—A man should speak the truth at all times and in all circumstances in pain and happiness. It is better to practice truthfulness than to perform various religious ceremonies;

(vii) *Sushrusa* or service—Asoka expected all his subjects to be obedient to their parents, elders, teachers and other respectable persons;

(viii) *Sampritipatti* or support—Proper treatment to ascetics, dependents, inferiors, servants, slaves, relatives, dependent friends and needy acquaintances;

(ix) *Apichiti* or reverence—Respect for teachers;

(x) *Ahimsa* or non-violence—Non-injury to living creatures mentally or physically;

(xi) *Anarambho Prananam* or vegetarianism—Non-slaughtering of animals.

Thus, these ideals if followed correctly will lead one towards higher living. As these are the points common to all religions, so Asoka can hardly be accused of utilizing his vast resources in the interest of any particular creed. To him, therefore, goes the credit of initiating the policies of peace and universal religion rather than of war and aggression. Hence, though Asoka was an ardent follower of Buddhism, yet he was a Catholic enough to study either faith such as Jainism and adopt some features of them as commended themselves to him.

Asoka's Measures for Promotion of Buddhism

According to a view, he assumed monastic vows and robe while still exercising autocratic control over a vast empire. Hence, he was both a monk and a monarch. He made a depth study of Buddhist scriptures and undertook *Dharma Yatra* (tours of morality). In the year 249 B.C. Asoka made a solemn pilgrimage to the most sacred places in the Buddhist Holy Land. He started from Patliputra, the capital, and advanced towards north along the royal road to Nepal, the course of which is marked by five great monolithic pillars, through the districts now known as Muzaffarpur and Champaran. Then he turned towards west and first visited the famous Lumbini Garden, the birth place of Buddha. A pillar was erected there to preserve the memory of his visit and it stands to this day. In his pilgrimage he was accompanied by his guide and preceptor, Upagupta. He then took Asoka to Kapilavastu, the home of Buddha's childhood; to Sarnath, the place where Buddha first achieved success as a preacher; to Sravasti, where he overcame the powers of darkness; and to Kusinagara, where he died.

He spread the teachings of Buddha by issuing edicts, which not only propagated religion but also Asoka's ideas on society and governance. These edicts were written in different scripts for the common people, for easy understanding. Most of them were in Brahmi, which was common in most parts of the empire.

The edict thirteen was written in Greek language and the other bilingual edicts were written in Greek and Aramic. He believed that the king should look upon his subjects as a father treats his children.

He also built a large number of monasteries or *viharas* in the country for the *bhikshus* to live in. Asoka even gifted two caves in the Barabara hills to the Ajivikas.

He himself set an example for his subjects to follow. He gave up hunting and taking of meat. He ordered, by a royal decree that no animal was to be sacrificed for the royal kitchen.

He also appointed *Dhamma Mahamatras*, special type of officers, to supervise the peaceful functioning of the principles of *Dhamma*. Asoka sent his son, Mahendra to Sri Lanka to preach Buddhism there and it is because of his efforts that it got converted to a Buddhist country. He also sent Buddhist missioners to other south-east Asian countries.

Buildings

Asoka is remembered not only for his *Dhamma,* but also for his patronage to architecture. He was a great builder; the buildings of the Mauryan age put the travelers to mere astonishment because of their beauty, design and execution.

1. Asoka's Palace: The building was mostly that of wood, and so most of that could not come to us but the Greek writers have left us impressive accounts of them. When Fa-Hein, the first Chinese pilgrim, visited Pataliputra, the capital, at the beginning of the fifth century, the palace of Asoka was still standing. "The royal palace and halls in the midst of the city, which exist now as of old, were all made by the spirits which he employed, and which piled up the stones, reared the walls and gates, and executed the elegant carving and inlaid sculpture work, in a way which no human hands of this world could accomplish."

2. Stupas: The Buddhist traditions credit Asoka with building as many as 84,000 stupas all over India and Afghanistan. A stupa is a commemorative monument usually housing sacred relics associated with the Buddha or other saintly persons. It is a dome like structure which consists of a round base and is made of brick and stone. Some of these stupas still survive and the most important among them is Sanchi and Barhut in central India. They were enclosed and enlarged at later times.

3. Monasteries: Asoka is also credited to have built many monasteries and cave dwellings for the monks. The caves were cut out of hard rocks and their walls were highly polished that they still shine like a mirror. One example is Barabara hills near Gaya by order of Asoka for the use of the Ajivika ascetics.

4. Pillars: The art of sculpture reached a high watermark under Asoka. The massive monolithic sandstone pillars, which Asoka erected in large numbers throughout the home provinces of the empire, some of which are 50 feet in height, and about 50 tons in weight, are not only worthy monuments of his magnificence, but also of the highest interest as the earliest known examples of the Indian stone-cutter's art in architectural forms. Each pillar consists of a shaft or column, made of one piece of stone, found at Chunar, near Mirzapur in U.P., supporting a capital made of another single piece of stone. Asokan pillars at Rampurva, Lauriya Nandangarh and Sarnath are excellent examples of stone sculpture. According to R.C. Majumdar, "The capital of the Sarnath Pillar is undoubtedly the best of the series. The figures of four lions standing back to back, and the smaller figures of animals in relief on the abacus, all show a highly advanced form of art and their remarkable beauty and vigour have elicited the highest praise from all the art-critics of the world." Many other pillars of Asoka, though inferior to that of Sarnath, possess remarkable beauty.

5. **Inscriptions:** The most interesting monuments of Asoka are his famous inscriptions, engraved upon rocks, cave-walls and pillars. They are more than thirty in number and supply the only safe foundation for the history of his reign. They give us insight into his inner feelings and ideals.

(i) There are Fourteen Rock Edicts, which according to Dr. Smith were engraved between 258-256 B.C. Most of them deal with his tours, Ahimsa, principles of Dhamma and appointment of Dhamma Mahamatras.

(ii) The Seven Pillar Edicts, according to V.A. Smith, must be read along with the Fourteen Rock Edicts, to which they refer, and of which they may be considered an appendix. They were issued in their complete form in or about the year 242 B.C., when Asoka was nearing the close of his career of activity in worldly affairs.

(iii) The three Cave Inscriptions at Barabara hills are merely brief dedications of costly cave dwellings for the use of a monastic sect known as Ajivika. These records are chiefly of interest as a decisive proof that Asoka was sincere in his solemn declaration that he honoured all sects; for the Ajivikas were extreme fatalists, having little or nothing in common with the Buddhists.

Hence, it is clear from the above that in the Mauryan period stone culture dramatically emerged as the principal medium of Indian artist. The art during Mauryan era reached the advanced stage of development in the evolution of Indian art.

Lion Capital of Ashoka

Source: Wikipedia

The famous original sandstone sculpted Lion Capital of Ashoka preserved at Sarnath Museum which was originally erected around 250 B.C. atop an Ashoka Pillar at Sarnath. The angle from which this picture has been taken, minus the inverted bell-shaped lotus flower, has been adopted as the National Emblem of India showing the Horse on the left and the Bull on the right of the Ashoka Chakra in the circular base on which the four Indian lions are standing back to back. On the far side there is an Elephant and a Lion instead. The wheel "Ashoka Chakra" from its base has been placed onto the centre of the National Flag of India.

Sanchi Stupa, Madhya Pradesh

Ashokan Pillar at Vaishali

Courtesy ASI

Asoka's Administration

Asoka is remembered in history as a philanthropic administrator. In the history of India, Asoka is referred to as Samraat Chakravartin Asoka—the "Emperor of Emperors Asoka". In his edicts, he is also referred to Devanampiya (beloved of the god) and Piyadasin (one who regards everyone with affection).

The administrative system during Asoka remained more or less the same as it was under his grandfather Chandragupta. The central and provincial administration was still run on the lines as were laid down the first Mauryan monarch. Asoka's style of administration is clearly stated in many edicts issued by him. The king was still the fulcrum of the central structure and was assisted by a council of ministers called *mantriparishad.* The central province with its capital Pataliputra was under the direct control of Asoka while the other few provinces were put under the charge of Viceroys who were princes of the royal family. The local and the municipal administration saw very little changes. Under him the welfare activities were increased.

Reforms Introduced in Administrative Structure

(i) **Introduction of New Idea to Save His Empire:** According to some historians, during the later half of the Asoka's reign, the expansion of the empire was almost complete. As Asoka ruled at a large empire it was comprised of people belonging to different social, cultural and religious groups. In order to avoid tensions arising out of these differences, he could have opted for two options: maintaining a huge army to check the disturbances which meant increased burden on the crown's exchequer or to opt for peaceful resolution. Asoka chose the second alternative to cement the gaps of divergent groups and maintain peace and harmony in his empire. Hence, he discovered the policy of *Dhamma.*

(ii) **Religious Toleration:** Asoka though himself was a great believer of Buddha, yet he did not force his belief on his subjects. He was completely tolerant towards other religions as well. He exhorted his subjects to exercise self-control and avoid criticizing any faith merely from attachment to one's own so that there may be a growth in mutual reverence and toleration. (Rock Edict XII).

(iii) Humanitarian Work: Asoka undertook the humanitarian work on a large scale. He was the first king in history who had established hospitals not only for men but also for animals. Medical herbs were planted for curing the various diseases of the suffering humanity. He declared that all his subjects were like his children and he desired their happiness in this and the other world. Asoka issued orders to all the officials to follow his example of serving the humanity. In the Pillar Edict IV he says, "As a man would make over his child to a skilful nurse and feel confident, says to himself, the skilful nurse is eager to care for the happiness of my child, ever so many governors have been created for the welfare of and happiness of the country."

(iv) Encouraging Periodical Tours: Asoka asked his officials to make periodical tours in their respective areas to know the actual status of his people and could hence easily solve their problems. He himself undertook periodical tours of his empire to check if the officials appointed are performing their duties properly. This method proved to be very beneficial as it brought the subjects and their ruler closer to each other. Asoka said that the king is expected to be agile and accessible to his officials at all times. In one of his edicts Asoka declared that even common people could meet him anytime.

(v) Appointment of Dhamma Mahamatras: New officials named as Dhamma Mahamatras were appointed as incharge of the new religion created by Asoka. They looked after the interest of the various religious communities, distributed charities among deserving persons and saw to the welfare of the state officials so that they did not harass the people. It was also their duty to see that justice was dispensed properly and that the people were leading their lives according to the law of *Dhamma*.

Asoka's Character

The edicts reveal Asoka as a combination of piety of a monk with wisdom of a king. He is the most remarkable personalities in the history of Ancient India. Asoka was not only a great conqueror but has also served humanity with his doctrine of *Dhamma*. He was vigorous and effective in his actions and propagated his creed and system of moral principles with absolute honesty. Every man, he maintained must work out for his own salvation. As recorded on Minor Rock Edict I "Let small and great exert themselves". The king and officials could only point out the road, which each man must travel for himself. Asoka was enthusiastic in his exertions and diligent in his passion of welfare of his subjects. He regarded all his subjects equal and was always ready to serve them. He asked his officials to look forward to him for humanitarian works. From 259 B.C. Asoka abolished the royal hunt which his predecessors and even he initially enjoyed. He even forbade the slaughtering of animals for royal kitchen. He preached and practiced the virtues of compassion, reverence, truthfulness, and sympathy. He was a man of affairs, versed in the arts of peace and war, the capable ruler of an immense empire, a great man, and a great king. He stands for non-violence and universal peace. He devoted his vast resources for the moral and spiritual enlightenment of his subjects. He realized that the true glory and fame of a king rested not upon the physical extent of his dominion but upon the moral progress which he could secure for his people. Thus, Asoka is considered to be one of the greatest monarchs not only of India but of the world also.

Asoka's Successors

The successors of Asoka could not maintain the integrity of the previous rulers of the Maurayan Empire. The *Vayu,* which is one of the oldest Puranas, gives only nine names for the Maurayan dynasty. And also states the duration of each reign. It even mentions that the total length of reigns of Maurayan dynasty is 133 years. The approximate dates are assigned by assuming that Asoka ruled for about forty or forty-one years. However, the Puranas assign 137 years to the Maurayan dynasty. Not much is known about the later Maurayans. If the Puranic tradition is to be believed, the immediate successor of Asoka was his son Kunala. The Kashmir tradition named Jalauka, another son of Asoka as his successors in that valley. Although a shadowy personage, he has more appearance of reality than Kunala. Tivara the third son of Asoka mentioned in the Queen's Edict, is not heard of again, and may have predeceased his father. None of Asoka's sons succeeded him in Patliputra. Perhaps the empire was divided immediately after Asoka's death, between his grandsons, Dasaratha taking the eastern, and Samprati the western provinces, but there is no clear evidence to support this hypothesis. The Buddhist prose romance, named Asokavadana (being part of the Divyavadana) tells why and how Samprati, son of the blinded Kunala, is placed on the throne. The Jain literary tradition of western India, also recognizes Samprati as the immediate successor of Asoka. He has also been regarded as an eminent patron of Jainism. The successor of Dasaratha and Samprati was Salisuka. According to the Puranas, Devavarman, Satadhams and Brihadratha were the successors of Salisuka. The last king of the Maurayan empire was Brihadratha, who was treacherously assassinated by his commander-in-chief, Pushyamitra Sunga. He laid the foundation of a new dynasty named Sunga.

Decline of Mauryan Empire

The whole duration of the Maurya dynasty, according to Puranic authority, was 137 years, and if this period be accepted and evaluated from the accession of Chandragupta in 322 B.C., the dynasty must have come to end in 185 B.C., which date certainly is approximately correct. The Mauryan Empire which was spread over a large part of the Indian subcontinent and also included Kandahar in modern Afghanistan met its end gradually. The following were the causes for the downfall of the empire:

(i) **Privilege Given to Buddhism:** The fall of the Mauryan authority probably was due in large measure to a reaction promoted by the Brahmans, whose privileged position must have been seriously affected by the extreme favour which Asoka showed to the Buddhist monks. The Buddhist preached against the Brahmanical religion and it ritualism. But there is nothing in the records of Asoka that he was an enemy of the Brahmanas. He believed in the policy of Equality before law. But then this was also a great disadvantage to the Brahmanas as earlier they enjoyed superior position in the society.

(ii) **Decline in the Military Power of the Maurayas:** As Asoka started following Buddhism in his later years of life, which was against violence of any kind. Hence, he paid less attention to maintain a strong army. The advent of Buddhism declined the martial spirit and the army became weak. The policy of peace and non-violence was adopted and Asoka nullified the doctrine that the main aim of a king should be the aggression of territorial states by war.

(iii) **Weak Successors of Asoka:** The successors of Asoka were weak and could not withhold the vast empire built up by him. The Mauryan Empire not only included the territories of India but also some area in modern Afghanistan. None of his sons and grandsons had the potential to rule and protect such a big empire from internal conflicts and external aggressions. Moreover, the separatist tendencies were equally responsible. As after the death of Asoka his empire was divided by his successors in the areas of their influence. Hence, the empire started declining rapidly.

(iv) **Monarchist Policy:** It is further to add that the Maurayan Empire was based on the principles of monarchy. The concentration of power was in the hands of one person, i.e. the king. The Mauryan Empire was based on king's personal rules and not on law. So when weak kings came to power the centre became weak and hence fell.

(v) **The Indo-Greek Invasion:** Some writers are of the opinion that foreign invasions led to the disruption of the Mauryan Empire. Among them Greek invasion was the foremost one. The Bactrians and the Parthians started attacking India as they were aware of the richness of this country and the weak central authority. Thus, the Mauryan kings failed to check the foreign aggression.

(vi) **Inefficient Administration:** The Mauryan rule was despotic in nature. The empire being too vast was divided into provinces ruled by different governors. They carried on the administration according to their own will. Thus, in several cases they were suppressive and misgoverned their state. In addition to this the capital was not centrally located and in those days of slow and inappropriate transport system it was difficult to effectively manage the outlying provinces which were far away from the centre. Ultimately, it paved the way for the gradual disintegration of the empire.

(vii) Advantage Taken by Pushyamitra Sunga: There existed no definite law of succession as a result of which there was always a war of succession amongst the sons and grandsons. Due to this the administration became completely weak. Thus, taking advantage of the growing discontentment against the kings Pushyamitra Sunga captured the throne by murdering the last Mauryan king, Brihadratha and laid the foundation of a new dynasty.

Thus, we may conclude that a variety of reasons were responsible for the downfall of the Maurayn Empire. The chief among them was that the Maurayan Empire was based on the personality of powerful monarchs and not any law or constitution, so as they fell the central power weakened.

IMPORTANT QUESTIONS

1. What are the sources of the study of the history of the Mauryas?
2. Evaluate the nature of state control on economic activities during the Mauryan period.
3. Discuss the nature and content of Asoka's policy of *Dhamma*. How far it reflected the teachings of Buddhism? What was the impact of this policy?
4. "The Asoka's Dhamma was not a new religion but an amalgamation of all religions in India." Comment.
5. Point out the salient features of the Mauryan art.
6. Discuss the *Saptang* theory.
7. Examine the causes for the decline of Mauryan Empire.
8. Write about the various measures taken by Asoka in the promotion of Buddhism.

REFERENCES

Basham, A.L., *The Wonder That Was India*, Delhi: Surjeet Publications, 2007.

Chaurasia, R.S., *History of Ancient India* (*Earliest times to 1200 A.D.*), New Delhi: Atlantic Publisher, 2008.

E notes, National Institute of Open Learning.

Jayapalan, N., *History of India* (*up to 1206 A.D.*), New Delhi: Atlantic Publishers, 2001.

Raychaudhuri, H.C., *An Advanced History of India*, New Delhi: Macmillan Publishers, 1978.

Smith, V.A., *The Early History of India*, New Delhi: Atlantic Publishers, 1999.

The Sunga, Kanva, and Andhra Dynasties (185 B.C.–225 A.D.)

9

SUNGA DYANSTY

Rise of Pushyamitra Sunga

Pushyamitra, the commander-in-chief, having killed his own master, Brihadratha Maurya, usurped the vacant throne and established a new dynasty in north India which in history is known by the name of Sunga. The people in general accommodated with the new dynasty as the later Mauryans had proved tyrannical and incompetent of stemming the tide of Greek invasion. The capital remained the same, Patliputra and perhaps his empire extended to the south up to *R.* Narmada. The Sunga dynasty probably assumed the territories in the Gangetic basin, corresponding with the modern Bihar, Tirhut, and the United Provinces of Agra and Oudh. It is unlikely that either the later Mauryas or the Sungas exercised any jurisdiction in the Punjab.

While the Sungas were ruling in north India, the Indo-Greeks (Yavanas) emerged in Bactria as an independent power and soon started extending their rule in the north-western and northern parts of India. Menander, a relative of the Bactrian monarch, and king of Kabul and the Punjab, advanced with considerable force into the interior of India. He achieved some success initially but later was pushed back with heavy losses by Pushyamitra Sunga. This is confirmed by Patanjali's *Mahabashya*. Pushyamitra ruled for 36 years. After him there were nine other rulers.

Successors of Pushyamitra

Pushyamitra was succeeded by his son the Crown Prince, Agnimitra. This prince is the hero of a famous drama

'Mahavikagnimitra' by Kalidasa. He in turn was succeeded by Vasujyeshtha, probably a brother, who was followed seven years later by Vasumitra. Vasumitra, the grandson of Pushyamitra Sunga, is said to have encountered and subdued a band of Yavanas (Greeks) during the reign of his grandfather. This is confirmed by the *Malavikaganimtiram* and *Gargi Samhita*. The next four reigns are said to have been abnormally short, amounting together to only seventeen years. The ninth king, Bhagavata, is credited with a long reign of thirty-two years, but we know nothing about him. The tenth king, was Devabhuti or Devabhumi, who ruled for ten years. Thereafter, there was a downfall of the dynasty and Kanva dynasty succeeded around 73 B.C. According to the Puranas, the Sunga dynasty's total reign lasted for 112 years.

Religious Attitude

Brahmanism witnessed revival during their rule. Pushyamitra even performed *asvamedha* sacrifice, which, according to immemorial tradition, could only be performed by a paramount sovereign. As per some Buddhist writers, Pushyamitra indulged in an unrestrained persecution of Buddhism, assassinating monks and burning monasteries. But some facts of his region clearly show that he did not persecute Buddhists. Interestingly, during the Sunga period the Sanchi Stupa was enlarged and faced with stones and decorated with railings, staircase and a harmika on the top. An inscription on the gateways of Barhut stupa assigns the work to King Dhanabhuti during the rule of the Sungas. This fact bears testimony to the high degree of tolerance prevailing during the period. Or, may be withdrawal of royal patronage with the coming of the Sungas apparently enraged the Buddhists and thus the Buddhists writers present an exaggerated account of their troubles.

Importance of the Sunga Period

In the field of literature, Sanskrit gradually gained ascendancy and became the language of the court. Patanjali was patronized by Pushyamitra Sunga and he was the second great grammarian of Sanskrit. Patanjali's Yoga Sutras and Mahabhasya were composed in this period. During the Sunga period, stone replaced wood in the railings and the gateways of the Buddhist stupas as noticed at Barhut and Sanchi. Barhut stupa is abundant with sculptures—apart from floral designs, animal figures, Yakshas and human figures. Even the stone railing around the Sanchi stupa is in rich belief work. This age definitely witnessed the increasing use of symbols and human figures in architecture. Even temple building began in this period. A Vishnu temple was built near Vidisha. There was an increase in the construction of rock-cut temple as noticed in the Chaitya Hall. In the temples and household worship, we find the idols of Shiva and Vishnu. The importance of the Sungas, therefore, was primarily in the context of cultural and social development. In the social field, the emergence of Hinduism had a wide impact.

KANVA DYANSTY

In 75 B.C. the last of the Sunga rulers, Devabhuti was killed treacherously by his minister Vasudeva, who then laid the foundations of the Kanva dynasty. The history of this dynasty is very obscure and perhaps no political event of historical importance happened during the reign of the Kanvas.

Absence of Political Events

There were four rulers of the Kanva dynasty who ruled only for 45 years (73-28 B.C.). Vasudeva was the founder of the dynasty. He ruled for nine years. The second ruler was Bhumimitra who ruled for about 14 years. The third king was Narayan who ruled for 12 years. The last king of the dynasty was Susharma who ruled for 10 years. Thus, this dynasty came to an end about by only after ruling for about 45 years. The Kanvas are spoken of in the Puranas as Sunga Bhartiyas. This suggests that although they usurped the supreme authority, yet allowed the puppet rulers of the Sunga line to rule in obscurity. In 50 B.C., the Kanvas as well as the puppet rulers of the Sunga line were swept away by the Satavahanas of the Deccan. The Satavahanas succeeded the Kanvas in eastern Malwa, while some princes with names ending in Mitra ruled in Magadha and Mathura. They were replaced by Saka Murandas and Satraps who in their turn were supplanted by the Nagas and the Guptas, who gave prominence to Hinduism.

Progress of Vedic Religion under Kanvas

The kings of Kanvas dynasty were followers of Brahmanism. They revived the religion and advanced state help. The result was that the spread of Buddhism at least was slowed down and there was gradual revival of Brahmanism. As such Hinduism became prominent and popular and religion of majority of people.

Downfall of Magadha Empire and Kanva Dynasty

The successors of Pushyamitra were weak and incapable rulers. Political unity of India ended. There were rebellions and being in distant provinces, the central government had become so weak that it could not suppress the revolts. The empire disintegrated gradually. In this way, the vast empire of Magadh was swallowed up by the Andhras or Satavahanas, Simuka the founder of the Andhra Empire ascended the throne in about 28 B.C. after the assassination of Susarman the last ruler of the Kanva dynasty.

THE ANDHRA OR SATAVAHANAS

Earliest Mention of the Andhras

During the days of Chandragupta Maurya, the Andhra nation, a Dravidian people, now represented by a large population speaking Telugu language, occupied the deltas of the Godavari and Krishna rivers on the eastern side of India. Megasthanese has described them as a powerful people with 30 walled towns and having a large army. The nation thus described undoubtedly was independent, and it is not known at what time, in the reign of either Chandragupta or Bindusara, the Andhras were urged to submit to the powerful forces at the command of the Maurya kings and recognize the sway of Magadha. The Andhras were not slow to take advantage of the opportunity given by the death of the great emperor, and very soon after the close of his reign, or possibly even before its close, set up as an independent power under the government of a king named Simuka.

Rise of Satavahanas

The founder of this dynasty was Simuka. Not much is known about Simuka, except that he subverted the Kanvas and the remnants of the Sunga power. Simuka was succeeded by his brother Krishna or Kanha. The new dynasty extended its sovereignty with such extraordinary rapidity that, in the reign of the second king, Krishna, the town of Nasik, near the source of the Godavari in the Western Ghats, was included in the Andhra dominions, which thus stretched across India. According to some *Puranas*, there were 19 rulers of this family who ruled for about 300 years. The Satavahana kingdom was wiped out in the first quarter of the third century A.D. (225 A.D.). Almost the whole of present-day Maharashtra, Madhya Pradesh and South India were under Satavahana rule. Paithan in Maharashtra, formerly called Pratishthan, was the capital of the Satavahanas. The Andhra kings all claimed to belong to the Satavahana family, and many of them bore the name of Satakarni. They are often mentioned without their personal name and it is thus sometimes impossible to ascertain which king is referred to.

Important Rulers of the Andhras

The third ruler Satkarni was an important ruler. He was a nephew of Krishna. He was a great conqueror who added to the empire Berar, Malwa, Central India and Hyderabad. Thus, his empire was a very vast one which included Saurashtra, Malwa, Berar, Konkan and the region near Poona and Nasik. Satkarni laid the foundation of his near capital Pratisthana in the Hyderabad state. He entered into a matrimonial alliance with the Marathi Chieftain of Western Deccan and conquered Eastern Malwa. He asserted his position as a paramount power by performing the Asvamedha Yajna or the horse sacrifice. He was probably the monarch who was defied by Kharavela king of Kalinga. After Satakarni the Andhras appear to have suffered a great setback because of the rise of the Sakas. Consequently, we do not know much about the successors of Satkarni for about a century.

Gautamiputra Satkarni

It was Gautamiputra Satkarni who restored the failure of the Satavahanas and raised their power and prestige to a great height. His first achievement was to recover Maharashtra. Then he waged successful wars against the foreigners defeating the Kshaharata Satrap, Nahapana and destroyed the power of the Sakas, Yavanas and the Pahalavas (Parthians). He built up an empire which extended from south to Malwa in the north. This Satakarni is known to us largely because of an inscription recorded at Nasik by his mother Gautama Balasri who sets forth his achievements. He dedicated a cave at Pandulena near Nasik in the 18th year of his reign and granted a field to certain ascetics. His reign period is noted by some scholars from 106 to 130 A.D.; he is credited with a rule of 24 years. He is considered as a very great ruler. His son, Vasishtiputra Pulumayi, ruled at Paithan on the banks of Godavari.

Pulumayi

Gautamiputra was succeeded by his son Pulumayi who reigned from 130 to 154 A.D. From the evidence of coins it appears that he was the first Satvahana ruler who extended his authority to the Andhra country. He married the daughter of Rudradaman the Saka Satrap of Ujjain but this relationship did not prevent war and he was twice defeated by his father-in-law. Some scholars held that the defeated monarch was not Pulumayi but his brother Vasisthiputra Satkarni and it was he that was Rudradaman's son-in-law. Sri Pulumayi died in about 155 A.D. A cave inscription in Kanheri refers to the queen of Vasishtiputra Satkarni as the daughter of Rudradaman. Due to the defeat he sustained at the hands of his father-in-law he lost a part of his father's empire.

Yagya Shri Satkarni

The last great ruler of the Andhras was Yagya Shri Satkarni who is regarded as the greatest of the last seven kings of the Andhras. He greatly recovered the partitions of the territory that were lost to the Sakas under Pulumayi and his other weak successors. He ruled a vast empire which extended from the Bay of Bengal in the east to the Arabian sea in the west. The discovery of a coin bearing the figure of a ship clearly indicates the existence of active maritime activity under Yagya Shri Satkarni. He is said to have ruled for about thirty years (165-195 A.D.). After the death of Yagya Shri Satkarni, the power of the Satvahanas declined. The history of the fall of the dynasty is obscure. The continued hostility of the Sakas weakened the empire. As a consequence the feudatories and military governors of the provinces were encouraged to set up independent rule in their own jurisdiction. Thus, the empire broke up.

Religious Conditions

The Andhra kings were Brahmanical Hindus but it is noteworthy that most of their recorded donations were made to Buddhist institutions. Satavahana kings were the first in Indian history to make tax free land grants to Buddhists and Brahmanas to gain religious merit. This practice became more prominent in succeeding periods. Princes and even ordinary citizens compete with one another in founding asylum and rest houses for the Buddhist monks.

The Satvahana kings claimed to be Brahmanas and considered it their primary duty to uphold *varna* system, i.e. the four-fold division of social structure. Hinduism was also very popular. The worship of Shiva and Vasudeva was widespread amongst the people.

Art and Literature

The Andhra kings were also great patrons of art and literature. Under this the Prakrit language made a great progress. One of their rulers Hala is said to have written the famous *Saptsalaka* in Prakrit. About the same time Gunadhya is said to have written his original *Birbatkatha* in Prakrit. Sarvevarman produced the *Katantra* for the benefit of an Andhra king who was ashamed of his ignorance of Sanskrit and found Panini too difficult.

IMPORTANT QUESTIONS

1. Describe the origin of the Sungas. Make an assessment of the achievements of Pushyamitra Sunga.
2. Give the importance of Sunga period.
3. Give the character and achievements of Gautamiputra Satkarni.

REFERENCES

Chaurasia, R.S., *History of Ancient India (Earliest times to 1200A.D.)*, New Delhi: Atlantic Publishers, 2008.

Directorate of School Education, *Higher Secondary Textbook of Tamil Nadu.*

E notes, National Institute of Open Learning.

Raychaudhuri, H.C., *An Advanced History of India*, New Delhi: Macmillan Publishers, 1978.

Smith, V.A., *The Early History of India*, New Delhi: Atlantic Publishers, 1999.

The Indo-Greeks, the Sakas, the Parthian, and the Kushanas

10

Introduction

With the collapse of the Mauryan Empire, Indian history for the time being loses its unity. There rise a number of new regional kingdoms in different parts of the country. At the same time, we witness invasions by various groups of people based in Central Asia and western China. These were Indo-Greeks, the Scythians or the Shakas, the Parthians or the Pahlavas and the Kushanas. It was through such political processes that India came in closer contact with the Central Asian politics and culture.

THE INDO-GREEKS

The most important advancement in the post-Mauryan period was the arrival of foreign tribal groups into India. Most of these belonged to the category of Indo-Greeks, while some groups came from Iran and Afghanistan and also China. They came to settle on the northern-western borders of India with Bactria (area to the northwest of the Hindukush mountains in the present-day north Afghanistan) as an important centre. The rulers of Bactria came to be called the Bactrian-Greeks because of their Hellenistic (Greek) ancestry. The Indo-Greeks were the first rulers in India to issue coins that can definitely be attributed to kings.

Demetrius was the son of Euthydemos, and son-in-law of Antiochos. Demetrius I started the conquest of the Indo-Kush and North-East India in about 200 B.C., establishing the Graeco-Indian (or Indo-Greek) Kingdom. He received the title of "King of India" following his victories south of the Hindu-

Kush. Demetrius governed together, the new kingdom which expanded progressively to a large portion of Afghanistan, Sind and Punjab. According to some scholars, he ruled from about 190 B.C. to about 167 B.C., when he was killed by Eukratides, who then became the king. The distant wars in India left little time for Demetrius to keep hold on Bactria, which gave an opportunity to one Eukratides for successful rebellion. He made himself master of Bactria in about 175 B.C. and became involved in many wars with the surrounding states and tribes, which he carried on with varying fortune and unvarying spirit. These states continued to flourish under the successors of Demetrius and Eukratides for many centuries in the Northwest of India.

Menander

The most important of the Greek rulers of Bactria, Menander (155-130 B.C.), conquered much of northern India. The Greek historians, include him among the Bactrian Greeks "who conquered more tribes than Alexander [the Great]". His empire appears to have included southern Afghanistan and Gandhara, the region west of the *R.* Indus. He reigned gloriously at Sakala, identified with modern Sialkot in the Punjab. His coins have been found at Kabul and Broach also called as Bharuch. He has been identified with king Milinda mentioned in the famous Buddhist text the *Milinda-panha* ("The Questions of Milinda"), which contains philosophical questions that Milinda asked Nagasena (the Buddhist author of the text) and informs us that impressed by the answers, the king accepted Buddhism as his religion. The wheel engraved on some of Menander's coins is probably connected with Buddhism. Some scholars identify him with Greek invader whom Pushyamitra Sunga repulsed. Menander was celebrated as a just ruler, and when he died was honoured with magnificent obsequies.

Antialcidas

Antialcidas Nikephoros was another famous king of the Indo-Bactrians, who reigned from his capital at Taxila. He is said to have sent a Greek ambassador, Helidorous to the count of Sunga ruler Kasiputra Bhagabhadra. Antialcidas is also known through his plentiful coins. He issued a number of bilingual Indian silver coins. Antialcidas is known from an inscription left on a pillar (the Heliodorus pillar), which was erected by his ambassador Heliodorus at the court of the Sunga king Bhagabhadra at Vidisha, near Sanchi. It states that he was a devotee of Krishna, the Hindu god.

Heliokles, the son of Eukratides, who had obtained Bactria as his share of his father's extensive dominion, was the last king of Greek race to rule the territories to the north of the Hindu Kush.

Effect of Greek Contact

The Greeks first came into touch with India at the time of Alexander's invasion, though he could not materially change the course of Hindu society. Then came Seleukas Nikator in about 306 B.C. But he got no chance to circulate the seeds of Greek culture on Indian soil. His aims were effectively checked on the frontiers by Chandragupta Maurya. The later expeditions of Demetrius, Eukratidas, Menander, etc. (*c.* 190-155 B.C.) penetrated far into the interior of the country. These were not merely raids. They led to the establishment of Greek rule which lasted for about 150 years. We learnt much from the Greeks in regard to coinage. They introduced the practice of using regular coins in place of rude marked coins. In literature the poetry of Homer was translated and sung by the Indians. In the stream of Astronomy the Indians are certainly indebted to the Greeks. Many Greek scholars came to India with Alexander and wrote on Indian history, which are relevant in constructions of contemporary socio-religious aspect. Greek invasion also helped in increased trade contacts between the two countries.

Indo-Greek Coins, courtesy RBI monetary museum

THE PARTHIANS OR THE PAHLAVAS

The foreign conquerors who superseded the Greeks in north-west India belong to three main groups, namely Sakas, Pahlavas or Parthians and Yue-Chi or Kushans. The Parthians were Iranian people and because of strong cultural association with the Shakas, these groups were accredited in the Indian sources as Shaka-Pahlava. Greek political power in the region west of *R.* Indus, was soon warned by the Parthians led by Mithradates I, a contemporary of Eukratides who ruled in the second century B.C. (*c.* 171-136 B.C.). He was a very able monarch, who succeeded in extending his dominions so widely that his power was felt as far as the Indus, and probably even to the east of that river. The famous *Takht-i-Bahi* inscription dated to 45 A.D. recovered from Mardan near Peshawar bespeak of the Parthian rule in north-western area of Pakistan. This inscription refers to the most important ruler of this dynasty Gondophares. Some literary sources associate him with St. Thomas, who is said to have converted both, the king and his brother, to Christianity. After his death the Parthian Kingdom was divided amongst many petty chieftains who were always busy quarrelling with each other. Its result was that a great part of the Parthian Kingdom was annexed by the Kushans in their own empire. Some of the Parthian chiefs remained on the Indian border for many centuries yet they ceased to be a political power. They lost importance due to rise of Kushans as a great power.

THE SAKAS OR THE SCYTHIANS

'Saka' is the Indian term used for the people called Scythians, who originally belonged to a nomadic tribe of Central Asia. But in about 165-160 B.C. they were driven out of their land by another powerful tribe called *Yueh-chi*. They in turn pounced down on the Bactrian and Parthian empire. As more and more Sakas came, the earlier ones were pushed forward and some of them crossed the Hindukush and the Suleiman ranges. Hence, they gradually came to settle in north-western India around Taxila in the first century B.C. Under the successive Saka rulers their territories extended up to Mathura and Gujarat. The Saka-Pahlava kings ruled over an empire that embraced several provinces. The governors of these administrative units were known as *Satraps* (Kshatrapa). This title was so much liked by the Sakas that even when they became independent rulers they continued to be called *Satraps*. This dynasty lasted until it was destroyed by Chandra Gupta II, Vikramaditya, about 390 A.D.

Saka Kings

The earliest of these Indo-Parthian kings apparently was Maues which is perhaps identical with Moga of Taxila Plate of Satrap Patika. He attained power in the Western Punjab perhaps about 120 B.C., and adopted the title of 'Great King of Kings' on his coins. Maues was succeeded by Azes I about 90 B.C. who conquered the eastern Punjab from the Greeks. He thus, completed the Saka conquest of the Greek territory in the Punjab. He struck coins on which the name of his successors was imprinted. Azes I was succeeded by his son Azilises and then by his grandson Azes II. Azes I certainly was a powerful prince, and enjoyed a long reign, perhaps extending to half a century. Azilises and Azes II also seem to have enjoyed a prolonged tenure of power.

The most famous of all the Saka rulers was Rudradaman who ruled in the middle of second century A.D. His empire was spread over almost whole of western India. His achievements are known through the only inscription that he got engraved on a boulder at Girnar or Junagarh. This inscription happens to be the first royal inscription of early India composed in chaste Sanskrit. He was a great patron of art and literature. He was a perfect master in such subjects as grammar, polity, music and polity. He never killed men except in battles. He acted more or less like a constitutional monarch and acted on the advice of his ministers. An important event in his reign was the repairs of the Sudarshna lake which had over flooded its banks and broken the embankments.

Decline

We have a long list of Rudradaman successors who continued to rule till the time of the Guptas. But their power gradually declined owing to disputed successions, internal feuds and attacks of powerful neighbours. Power gradually fell into the hands of Aphire chieftains. After Rudradaman's death in about A.D. 140, his seventeen successors tried to maintain their ancestral kingdom but ultimately their state was annexed by the rising Gupta's in the fourth century A.D. Greeks and Sakas who remained in India became integral part of Indian society and culture.

THE KUSHANA EMPIRE

The Kushanas, originally belonged to western China. They are also called as Yueh-chis. The Chinese historians inform us that there were five clans or tribes of the Yueh-chi of which the Kushans were one. The Kushanas after defeating Sakas and Pahlavas created a big empire over Kabul, Kandhar, and Afghanistan. The first prominent ruler of the Kushana dynasty was Kujula Kadphises or Kadphises I. He is said to have ruled for about thirty years from 15 A.D. - 45 A.D. He was succeeded by his son Wema Kadphises also known as Kadphises II. He was a great warrior like his father. He defeated the Saka Kshatraps and extended the Boundaries of his empire up to Banaras. Next ruler was Kanishka. He was the most famous of the Kushanas.

Kujula Kadphises

The pressure of population upon the means of subsistence, which had impelled the Yueh-chis to undertake the long and formidable march from the borders of China to the Hindu Kush, now drove it across that barrier, and stimulated Kadphises I to engage in the formidable task of subjugating the provinces to the south of the mountains. His empire extended from the frontiers of Persia to the Indus, with probably all the territories comprised in the existing kingdom of Afghanistan. At the age of eighty Kadphises I closed his victorious reign, and was succeeded, in or about 45 A.D., by his son, who is most conveniently designated as Kadphises II.

Kadphises II

He was equally ambitious and enterprising like his father, and devoted himself to the further extension of the Yueh-chi dominion. He conquered the Punjab and a considerable part of the Gangetic plain, probably as far as Benares. He then set up generals, who governed in his name. The Lower Sind continued under the rule of Parthian chiefs. Kadphises II issued gold coins which showed the wealth and prosperity of his kingdom. His coins show that he was a worshipper of Siva and called himself Maheswara. He had maintained friendly relations with the Roman Empire. The discovery of the large number of Roman coins of that period in India clearly indicates that there existed very close commercial relations between India and the Roman Empire during the reign of Vima Kadphises. The Roman gold began to pour in India in exchange for the Indian goods such as silk, spices and various other articles. Vima is said to have ruled for about thirty-three years from 45 A.D.-78 A.D.

Kanishka

Kadphises II was succeeded by Kanishka, who alone among the Kushana kings has left a name cherished by tradition, and famous far beyond the limits of India. Kanishka is treasured as a great patron of Buddhism. He has been credited for calling the fourth voluminous Buddhist council in Kashmir which marked the beginnings of Mahayana Buddhism. He is among the legends of Tibet, China, and Mongolia, and is scarcely less significant to the Buddhists of those lands than that of Asoka himself. During his regime there was also a voluminous increase in trade and exchange of ideas with Roman Empire via Silk Road.

Our knowledge is so limited that difficulties remain, in regard to when Kanishka came to power. It is not known what his connection was with Vima Kadphises. There are several views about Kanishkas date of accession. J. Fleet, V.A. Smith and R. Majumdar respectively suggest that Kanishka ascended the throne in 58 B.C., 125 A.D. and 248 A.D. But the general accepted view about his accession is 78 A.D. as suggested by R.D. Banarjee and H.C. Roy Choudhury, etc. But few evidence lead to the conclusion that Kanishka came to the throne late in the first century of the Christian era, and most probably in 78 A.D. directly succeeding Kadphises II. Tradition, inscription and the monuments of his time prove that his government through inheritance and conquest, extended all over North-western India, as far as the Vindhyas in south, as well as over the remote regions beyond the Pamir passes. Thus, Kanishka built and enjoyed one of the largest empires both in India and Asia in ancient time. According to famous traveler Hiuen Tsang, the capital of Kanishka was Purushpura (Peshawar). He was the founder of the Saka era which begins from 78 A.D.

Conquests of Kanishka

He is known in history as a hardy warrior whose rule extended not only over Indian territories but also over modern Afghanistan and some parts of Central Asia. Hiuen Tsang recognized Kanishka's sovereignty over Gandhara, Oudh, Benaras and his capital at Peshawar. *Rajtarangini* (a text on history of Kashmir) by Kalhana acknowledged the rule of Kanishka over Kashmir. He certainly showed a marked preference for that delightful country, where he erected numerous monuments, and founded a town, which, although now reduced to a petty village, yet bears his honoured name. It was here that Kanishka called the fourth magnificent Buddhist Council. Kanishka wanted to establish his sway in all directions and this could not be brought without defeating the Sakas of Punjab and Mathura. It is ever believed that he defeated the Saka Kshatrapas of Ujjain and wrested from them some territories of their empire. Tradition affirms that he penetrated far into the interior of India, and attacked the king residing at the ancient imperial city of Patliputra. It is said that he carried off from this city a Buddhist saint named Asvaghosha, who wrote the *Buddha Charita*.

The ambition of Kanishka was not confined by the limits of India. He is alleged to have engaged in successful war with the Parthians, having been attacked by the king of that nation. The most striking military exploit of Kanishka outside India was his conquest of Kashgar, Yarkand, and Khotan, part of mighty Chinese Empire. He failed in his first expedition in 90 A.D. and was defeated by the Chinese general Pan-chao. But after the death of Pan-chao, succeeded in his second expedition, and freed himself from the obligation of paying tribute that he had been paying since the time of his first expedition to the Chinese emperor. According to tradition, Kanishka subdued three regions but could not subdue the north.

Administration

Kanishka was not only a great conqueror but also a very good administrator. He no doubt ruled like a despotic monarch but never ignored the welfare of his people. Very less is known about his administration. Though the Sarnath inscription mentions that he divided his empire into many provinces for administrative convenience and placed them under the charge of Kshatrapas. Some of those provinces were Khotan, Yarkand, Kashgar, Bactria, Afghanistan, Punjab, Sind, Kashmir and Mathura, etc. The Sarnath inscription mentions Kharara Pallana as the Kshatrap of Mathura, Benaras and the eastern regions. The viceroys or Kshatrapas were appointed very carefully and were embedded with power to look after trade and business. Every care was taken to maintain perfect peace and order in the empire. Anyone who tried to revolt was severely dealt with. The capital of Kanishka was one of the most beautiful cities of India at that time and was adorned with many noble public buildings and Buddhist monasteries, etc. Sources indicate that Kushana horsemen wore trousers while riding. A headless statue of Kanishka found at Mathura reflects the same.

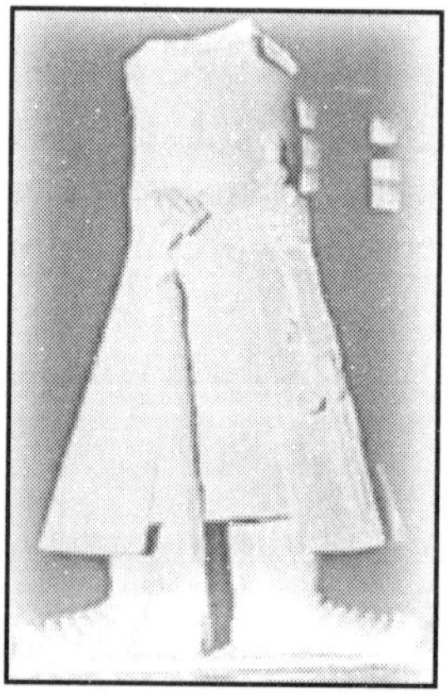

Headless statue of Kanishka, Mathura museum

Kanishka and Buddhism

It is not his conquest and administration but the patronage he extended to Buddhism that he is famous for in history. The Buddhist traditional texts refer Kanishka as second Asoka to their religion. His personal faith was Buddhism is evident by the *chaitya* that he got constructed at Peshawar, which was much admired by the travellers. The reign of Kanishka is specially celebrated for the convocation of a Buddhist council, organized on the model of that summoned by Asoka. He studied the Buddhist scriptures in his leisure time under the guidance of a monk.

Kanishka's zeal for Buddhism did not make him intolerant of the other creeds followed by this numerous subjects all over his empire. His coins show that he honoured the Zoroastrian, Greek, and Brahmanic deities as well as the Buddha. The Buddhist texts affirm that in his early life Kanishka also involved in impious acts like Asoka but subsequently adopted Buddhism under the influence of Asvaghosa owing to the profound remorse for his past misdeeds. The most authentic evidence on the subject of his change of faith is afforded by the long and varied series of his coins, which like most ancient coinages, reflect the religious ideas of the monarch. During later years of his life, his coins exhibit the images of Buddha with his name in Greek letters. As the Hinayana scriptures give honourable position to Asoka, the Mahayana scriptures gives credit to Kanishka.

The Buddhist Council

The reign of Kanishka is especially important in the history of Buddhist church. It is known from the traditions of Northern India, as preserved by Tibetan, Chinese, and Mongolian writers. Kanishka who studied Buddhist literature, became hopelessly baffled by the conflicting doctrines of the various sects, suggested to his adviser that it would be great to obtain an authoritative exposition of the truth. It was decided by all the learned men to convoke an assembly in the pleasant climate of Kashmir, at a monastery named Kundalavana. Vasumitra was the president and Asvaghosa, the vice-president. It was attended by 500 monks. The comprehensive commentaries were copied on sheets of copper, which were deposited in a stupa built for this purpose by the order of king Kanishka.

Rise of Mahayana

The early Buddhists regarded the master merely as a human being, a great guide in the journey of life. He was now raised to the position of God. This led to a doctrine of salvation by faith in Budhha. The rituals were also elaborated. This modified form of Buddhism was known as 'Mahayana' the great vehicle in contradiction to the Hinayana the little vehicle. Kanishka declared the Mahayana Buddhism as the state religion of his empire. The medium of Mahayana literature was Sanskrit.

Death of Kanishka

Kanishka is said to have met a violent death at the hands of his own people, as they were tired of his continued conquest and hard campaigns. Hence, when once he was ill, they covered him with a quilt, a man sat on top of him and the king died on the spot. His reign appears to have lasted some forty-five years, and may be assumed to have terminated about 123 A.D.

Successors of Kanishka

His immediate successor was Vasishka, who had a short reign and was succeeded by Huvishka. Vasudeva I was the last of the great Kushana kings. The inscriptions of Vasudeva I are mostly found at Mathura and indicate a reign of not less than twenty-five years. His coins are testimony to the fact that he was a marked devote of Lord Siva.

Contribution of the Kushanas

The name of Kushanas stands conspicuous in history for their contribution in the various fields of life. They were great patrons of art and literature. A large number of philosophers, poets, dramatists and scholars adorned their court. Asvaghosa, Vasumitra and Nagarjuna flourished during the reign of Kanishka. *Buddhacharita,* a full length biography of Gautam Buddha was written by Asvaghosa. There vast empire and better administration helped in the growth of not only internal but external trade. It was in their era that India had trade relations with Roman Empire. The prosperity and richness of the empire is best attributed by the large number of gold coins that they struck. Indians made progress even in the field of medicine. The Kushanas patronized the Gandhara and the Mathura schools of sculptural art which are known for producing the earliest images of Buddha and Boddhisattavas.

Kushana gold coins. *Courtesy*: RBI monetary museum

Decline of Kushan Power

Vasudeva I was the last Kushan king who continued to hold extensive territories in India. After his death there is no indication of the existence of a paramount power in northern India. Probably, numerous Rajas asserted their independence and formed a number of short-lived states such as commonly arise from the ruins of a great oriental monarchy. None of the dynasties thus emerged could claim paramount rank. The period between the extinction of the Kushan and Andhra dynasties, about 220 A.D. or 230 A.D., and the rise of the imperial Gupta dynasty, nearly a century later, is one of the darkest in the whole range of Indian history.

POST MAURYAN DEVELOPMENTS

Trade and Commercial Activities

The most important development in the post Mauryan period was the development in trade and commerce. Trade developed both internally and externally and via land and sea. The most important ports of India were Bharuch (Broach), Kalyana in the west, which facilitated trade with Roman Empire and Tamralipti (W. Bengal), Arikamedu (Tamil Nadu) coast in the east which conducted trade with South-east Asia. The sea trade increased more after the discovery of monsoons by Hippatus a Greek navigator in 45 A.D. The best account of Indo-Roman trade is given in the book called *Periplus of the Erythrean Sea*, written in the first century A.D. by an anonymous author. The Romans required Indian spices and fine textiles and exported gold and silver to India in return.

The craft industry also saw a tremendous increase in this era. Craft production saw specialization in various fields. The text called *Milindapanho* mentions more than 60 craft occupations. Bead making, gold jewelry, cotton and silk textiles, etc. were among those. Vanga (E. Bengal) became famous for silk textiles and Ujjain for bead making.

The different art and crafts led to an increase in the number of traders who organized themselves into groups called *shreni* or guilds. These were basically group of people pursuing the same profession or dealing in the same commodity. These people mutually decided the rules and regulations as regard the quality and price of the commodity. The head of the guild was known as *sreshthi.*

Emergence of Sculptural Art Schools

In the fourth council during the reign of Kanishka, Buddhism split into two major sects called Hinayana and Mahayana. Mahayana adopted Sanskrit as its language and started worshipping Buddha in the human form; as a result a large number of Buddha images were built in different regions. Hence, emerged three different sculptural arts: Mathura School of Art, Gandhara School of Art, and Amravati School of Art.

Mathura School of Art

It is a Buddhist art that flourished in the pilgrimage centre of Mathura, Uttar Pradesh from the 2nd century B.C. to the 12th century A.D. Its most distinctive contributions were made during the Kushan and Gupta periods (1st-6th century A.D.). It is undoubtedly the earliest Indian representation of Lord Buddha, as before that Buddha was always depicted by symbol such as a wheel, a throne, or a pair of footprints, and never by any human figure. The Mathura artists used local red stone with black spots to make the images. Mathura artists also yielded large number of images of Jaina deities. The Brahmanical influence on the art school is also evident, besides secular subjects. The images of Vishnu, Kartikeya and Kubera are the most noticeable among the brahmanical deities.

Gandhara School of Art

Gandhara School of Art was the next important stage in the growth of art and now the image of Buddha had become common. The Gandhara region was situated on the north-western part of the India. This region had been ruled by many dynasties such as the Mauryas, Sungas, Sakas, Greeks, and Kushanas for many centuries. However, the chief patrons of this art were the Sakas and the Kushanas. Probably, the Gandhara style had been originated under the Indo-Bactrian and Indo-Parthian rulers but it was under Kanishka that it made rapid developments. The artist used blue-grey stone to make idols of Buddha and Bodhisattava. This school has influence of Roman, Greek and Indian art and hence it is sometimes also known as Graeco-Roman, Indo-Greek or Graeco-Buddhist art. The chief feature of this art was the beautiful portrayal of human features with distinguished muscles of the body. Much attention was paid in depicting each and every drape of the garment. It was in Graeco-Roman fashion with very curly hair and beautiful representation of moustaches. Another important characteristic ot this school was that it attached more importance to refineness and polish of the statue. The techniques applied were Greek in nature but the ideas, inspiration and subjects were all Indian. According to R.C. Majumdar, "The Gandhara artist had the hand of a Greek but the heart of an Indian."[1] The image of Buddha was an imitation of Greek God *Apollo*. For a long time, it was believed that the Gandhara Buddha image served as the model for those executed at Mathura and other centres. But it is now recognized that the Buddha image was evolved independently at Mathura and Gandhara. The former stressed on the abstract and spiritual expression of the figure and the later on physical accuracy and beauty. It may be noted that both the art schools flourished under the lavish patronage of the Scythian kings.

Amravati School of Art

This art flourished under the Satvahanas and Ikshavaku rulers from 150 B.C. to 350 A.D. The Amravati school of art prospered in the region of Andhra Pradesh between the lower valleys of rivers Krishna and Godavari. The figures of Amravati school are vivacious and slim although are depicted in the most difficult poses. Sculptures of this school are also seen on the railings, pedestal and other parts of stupas. The Buddha is represented by symbols and themes. For example, one medallion depicts a whole story of 'taming of an elephant by the Buddha'.

IMPORTANT QUESTIONS

1. Outline the chief elements of different schools of Art which developed in the early centuries of the Christian era.
2. Discuss the invasion of Greeks on India in the 2nd century B.C. and after.
3. Who were the Kushanas? Describe the extension of the empire of Kanishka.
4. "Kanishka was as great to Buddhists as Asoka." Comment.
5. Write a note on the post Mauryan developments.

NOTE

1. R.C. Majumdar, *An Advanced History of India*, p. 228.

REFERENCES

Basham, A.L., *The Wonder That Was India*, Delhi: Surjeet Publications, 2007.

Chaurasia, R.S., *History of Ancient India (Earliest times to 1200 A.D.)*, New Delhi: Atlantic Publishers, 2008.

Encyclopedia Britannica.

E notes, National Institute of Open Learning.

Raychaudhuri, *An Advanced History of India*, New Delhi: Macmillan Publishers, 1978.

Smith, Vincent A., *The Early History of India*, New Delhi: Atlantic Publishers, 1999.

The Guptas and Their Successors (300 A.D.–550 A.D.)

11

Introduction

In the fourth century light again dawns, the guise of unconsciousness is lifted, and the history of India regains unity and interest. On the ruins of the Kushan Empire arise a new empire which established its sway over a good part of the former dominions of both the Kushanas and Satvahanas. This was the power of the Guptas. The Gupta dynasty ruled for about two centuries and under them the country made such a progress in all the fields that their period is known as the 'Golden Age' in Indian history.

Sources of Gupta History

1. Literary Sources: The Puranas, especially the *Vayu Purana*, *Matsya Purana*, *Vishnu Purana* and *Bhagwat Purana*, furnish important information regarding the Gupta reign. They provide relevant information about the polity of the time and the names of the provinces. They also tell us about the progress in the field of science in the Gupta period. But as these books are not written from historical point of view they can be best read by comparing them with other available sources. The *Kaumudi Mahotsava* is a drama in five Acts, which lays down the political condition of Magadha on the eve of ascendancy of the Guptas. Bana's *Harshacharita, Devichandraguptam* and works of Kalidasa are other important literary sources. They provide us with significant knowledge of the events of the Gupta period.

2. Chinese Traveller Accounts: Fa-Hein was the earliest Chinese pilgrim who visited India during the reign of Chandra

Gupta-II. He remained in India from 405 to 411 A.D. His work tells us the social, religious and economic condition of India at that time. He noted the wealth and prosperity of the towns and their citizens. He also refers to the free hospitals maintained by the state and other charitable institutions. Fa-Hein states that Vikramaditya was capable of bestowing on his people the benefits of orderly government in sufficient manner to allow them to grow rich in peace and prosper abundantly. He has given vivid picture of the country and society. Another Chinese traveler I-tsing, who travelled in India after the Gupta age refers to Maharaja Srigupta. He says that the Guptas had built a great temple near Mrigasikhanana for the Chinese pilgrims.

3. The Pillar Inscriptions: The most important source of information, regarding Samudragupta is the inscription that is found written on the Asoka Pillar which stands in the Allahabad Fort. The Allahabad Pillar inscription was written by Harisena, the court poet of Samudragupta and so it contains a first-hand knowledge about Samudragupta's reign, his power and achievements. The Iron Pillar of Mehrauli gives very useful information about Chandragupta Vikramaditya. It is a victory pillar which Vikramaditya set up after his great victory over the Vahlikas. The "Bhitari Pillar Inscription" of Skandagupta tells us about the fight with the Pushyamitras and probably also with the Hunas during the reign of his father Kumaragupta I.

4. Art: The discovery of a large number of works of art pertaining to the Gupta period has also proved very useful as regards the cultural history of India during the Gupta period. The art not only depicts different aspects of life but also illustrates different schools of art and architecture. The temples of the Gupta period give us an idea of the religious beliefs of the people. And the paintings of Ajanta and Ellora caves pointed the artistic tastes of the people.

5. Numismatics: A lot of useful and authentic information for the history of the Guptas is to be found in the coins of the Gupta emperors. A close study of these coins provides us with useful information regarding the artistic achievements, economic conditions and personal accomplishments of the Gupta rulers. The coins of Samudragupta bear the image of Vishnu and veena. These indicate his love for music and his religious ideas, etc.

Before the rise of the Gupta dynasty, Northern India was divided into a number of small monarchical kingdoms and republics. The Guptas were a local dynasty before they conquered the whole of Northern India. Srigupta is regarded as the founder of the Gupta dynasty, who probably belonged to the Vaishya caste. Srigupta was succeeded by Ghatotkacha, who appears to be some small king about whom nothing much is known. After Ghatotkacha, Chandra Gupta I succeeded him as the king. Nothing definite is said about the origin of the Guptas.

Chandra Gupta I (320-335 A.D.)

The real founder of the Gupta Empire was Chandra Gupta I (320 A.D.-334 A.D.). The year of his accession marks the beginning of the Gupta era. Chandra Gupta I in a breakthrough deal like the great Bimbisara, married Kumaradevi, a Lichchhavi princess from Nepal which strengthened his position. Kumaradevi must have brought to her husband's family an enormous accession of power and prestige. He took the title of *maharajadhiraja* (king of kings). This event is recorded in a series of gold coins issued by Chandra Gupta I. He also struck coins in the joint names of himself, his wife and his son. He ruled over Tirhut, South Bihar, Oudh, and modern Allahabad with his capital at Patliputra. He held an assembly to formally nominate his son, Prince Samudragupta as his successor to the imperial throne of the Guptas. Nothing is known about the death of Chandra Gupta I. Probably, after assigning the throne to Samudragupta, he became an ascetic and died as such.

King and Queen type coin. *Courtesy* RBI museum

Samudragupta (335–375 A.D.)

Before Chandra Gupta's death, which occurred perhaps about ten or fifteen years later his coming to the throne, he selected as his successor the Crown Prince, Samudragupta, his son by the Lichchhavi princess. Samudragupta followed a policy of conquest and enormously enlarged his kingdom. He had no hesitation in acting on the principle that 'kingdom taking' is the business of kings. He employed a learned poet Harisena in his court to write a glaring account of the military exploits in pure Sanskrit. The inscription is engraved on a Pillar at Allahabad Fort. The record composed survives practically to this day, although unfortunately, the document is not dated. It enumerates the people and the regions conquered by Samudragupta.

Samudragupta is probably the greatest of his house. He was popularly known as the "Indian Napoleon" as he conquered many territories without making much of an effort. In fact, he died unchallenged in the battlefield while Napoleon did not. It is said that after Emperor Asoka, the empire of Samudragupta was the supreme. The coins found in excavation reveal much information about his empire. He celebrated his conquests by performing *ashvamedha* (a horse sacrifice) and by issuing ashvamedha coins, the coins portraying the scene of sacrifice. His coins also exhibit his love for music, as few of his coins represent him as playing on a vina.

King as horseman. *Courtesy*. RBI monetary museum

His Campaigns

The conquests of Samudragupta are geographically classified under four heads: as those directed against eleven kings of the south, who were conquered and liberated; nine named kings of Gangetic plain who were defeated and whose kingdoms were annexed; the chiefs of the wild forest tribes situated in the Vindhya region, who were brought under the control of Samudragupta; and the rulers of the five frontier kingdoms and republican states, who agreed to pay tribute and taxes to Samudragupta and obey his orders without any fight. The inscriptions add that Samudragupta also received tributes from many kings of South-east Asia.

Limits of His Empire

The kingdom of Samudragupta in the middle of the fourth century comprised all the most populous and fertile countries of Northern India. It extended from the Hooghly on the east to the Jamuna and Chambal on the west; and the Himalayas in the north to the Narbada in the south. Beyond these wide limits, the frontier kingdoms of Assam and the Gangetic delta, as well as those on the southern slopes of the Himalayas, and the free tribes of Rajputana and Malwa, were attached to the empire by bonds of subordinate alliance; while almost all the kingdoms of the south had been overrun by the emperor's armies and compelled to acknowledge his irresistible might. Thus, he can rightly be called the Indian Napoleon because his conquests can be easily compared to that of Napoleon.

Relations with Foreign Powers

His empire was the largest since the days of Asoka, six centuries before, and its possession naturally entitled Samudragupta to the respect of foreign powers. He maintained diplomatic relations with the Kushan king of Gandhara and Kabul, and the greater sovereign of the same race who ruled on the banks of the Oxus, as well as with Ceylon and other distant islands. Samudragupta had developed very cordial relations with Ceylonese ruler Siri Meghavanna (Meghavarna). Gupta Empire was smaller than Mauryan Empire but its influence in foreign countries was as great as of Mauryan Empire and probably due to its influence Hinduism became popular in Indonesia and in Indo-Chinese countries.

Personal Accomplishments

The laureate mention his patron's proficiency in song and music, which has been confirmed by the existence of a few rare gold coins depicting his majesty comfortably seated on a high-backed couch, engaged in playing the Indian *veena*, a musical instrument. All the fine arts, music, dance, sculpture and architecture flourished well. Literature also reached its highest watermark in his times. According to V.A. Smith, "Samudragupta was a man of exceptional personal capacity and unusually varied gifts." The last part of Harisena's Prasasti refers to Samudragupta's sharp and polished intellect, his musical talents, and his title of *Kaviraja* a capacity which would secure a good livelihood for a poet. Sanskrit language received great royal patronage. The Guptas were staunch Hindus. Samudragupta himself worshipped Lord Vishnu and Lord Shiva, though he showed a spirit of tolerance to all the other faiths. He allowed the king of Ceylon to build a splendid Buddhist monastery at Bodh Gaya for the pilgrims. The royal support was extended to the revival of Hinduism. The performance of *asvamedha yajna* by Samudragupta indicates an influence of the Brahmanical Hinduism on him. *Ashvamedha yajna* also gave him the coveted title of Maharajadhiraj, the supreme king of kings. He gathered round himself a galaxy of poets and scholars, not the least eminent among who was the warrior-poet Harisena. Samudragupta like Asoka set in his mind the ideal of world-conquest by means of *parakrama*. As a warrior he occupies a very prestigious place not only in the history of India but also that of the world. He is so often compared with Napoleon and Alexander. He defeated nine rulers of the north and subjugated eleven kings of the Deccan. Wherever he went success greeted him. He was a versatile monarch.

Death

Samudragupta was conferred with no ordinary powers. He was a man of genius, who may adequately acquire the title of the Indian Napoleon. His personal appearance cannot be known sufficiently due to lack of resources. The exact year of Samudragupta's death is also not known, but it is certain that he lived to an advanced age, and enjoyed the reign for nearly half a century. Before he passed, he peacefully transmitted his crown by nominating his most worthy son, from Queen Datta Devi, as his successor.

Fa-Hein

Fa-Hein was a Chinese pilgrim who visited India in the beginning of the fifth century A.D. He left China in about 399 A.D. and reached India in about 405 A.D. after facing a good deal of hardships in the way. He came by land route. He stayed in India for about six years (405 A.D.-411 A.D.) and went back by the sea route visiting Ceylon, Java, and Sumatra on his homeward journey. During his stay in India he visited various important places such as Peshawar, Taxila, Mathura, Kapilvastu, Bodh Gaya, Sarnath, Kushinagar and Patliputra and all the holy places connected with the life of Sakyamuni. At Patliputra he stayed for about three years and his written in detail about the political, social, economic and religious conditions of India for those days under the Gupta monarch Chandragupta Vikramaditya who ruled from 380 A.D.-414 A.D. His views are reliable.

System of Administration: In contrast to the Mauryas the Gupta Kings adopted pompous titles such as 'Paramesvara', 'Maharajadhiraja' and 'Param Bhattaraka'. Kingship was hereditary. The throne did not always go to the eldest son. The Guptas made munificent gifts to the Brahmanas. The numerical strength of the Gupta army is not known. The king maintained a standing army, chariots receded into the background and cavalry came to the forefront. Horse archery became prominent in military tactics.

The king collected taxes varying from one-fourth to one-sixth of the produce. The villagers were subjected to forced labour for serving the royal army and officials.

Judicial System: The judicial system was far more developed under the Guptas than in earlier times. Civil and criminal laws were clearly defined and books compiled. Elaborate laws were laid down about inheritance. It was the duty of the king to uphold the law. The guilds of the artisans and merchants were guided by their own laws. Laws were just, punishment was mild, justice was fair, impartial, quick and unexpensive.

The most important affairs in the Gupta empire were assigned to the Kumaramatyas. They were appointed by the king in the home provinces and were paid in cash. The empire was divided into divisions (Bhuktis). Each Bhukti was under the charge of 'Uparika'. The Bhuktis were divided into districts and districts into 'Vithis' and villages. Religious functionaries were granted land free of tax for ever. The beneficiaries could collect from the peasants all the taxes. They were also empowered to punish the criminals. Much of the imperial administration was managed by the feudatories. The state did not take part in economic activities on any big scale as it did in Maurya time.

Economic Life: Fa-Hein informs us that Magadha was full of cities and its rich people supported Buddhism and gave charities. Till 550 A.D. India carried on trade with the Eastern Roman empire. The demand for Indian silk abroad slackened. There was decline of trade and rise of landed classes. The priestly landlords became very powerful. The Gupta princes were great supporters of the Brahmanical order. The priestly class accumulated wealth on account of numerous land grants.

Social Conditions: Fa-Hein writes that a wave of prosperity spread all over the country. The people enjoyed complete freedom of movement and there was no need of any passport whatsoever. The society was based on caste system. A large number of foreigners had been assimilated into the Indian society. The Hunas came to be recognised as one of the thirty-six clans of the Rajputs. In some ways, the position of Sudras and women improved in this period. They were now permitted to listen to the epics. The Guptas were staunch Hindus but they observed a spirit of toleration towards the people of other faiths. The people enjoyed perfect religious freedom. Buddhism was flourishing side by side with Hinduism. The monasteries were quite rich and possessed enough land. Chandragupta II issued many types of coins. The archer type, chhatra type, lion slayer type and horseman type coins were minted. On one coin the Garud has been shown on one side and goddess Lakshmi on the other.

Patliputra and Other Cities: Fa-Hein writes about the city of Patliputra, the capital of the Gupta Empire. It was a big city and was a great centre of learning art and religion. There were two large and beautiful Buddhist monasteries where about seven hundred monks were ever busy in imparting knowledge to the students who flocked from all parts of India and abroad. The Asoka's palace still retained all its splendour even after a lapse of six or seven centuries. It seemed that it was not the work of men but of spirits. The people were quite rich and prosperous. "They left behind one another in the practice of benevolence and sighteousness." They organised a grand procession in honour of Lord Buddha every year. There were free hospitals for the poor in which food and medicines were given free of cost. There were also rest houses in large towns as well as on the national highways for the benefit of the travellers and traders.

Indian Shipping and Overseas Relations: Fa-Hein has left behind him very valuable information regarding Indian shipping and overseas relations. He writes that trade was carried on both in India and in foreign lands by land as well as sea routes. Gambay and Baroach had become very important because of their trade relations with China and Ceylon, East Indies and European countries.

Art: The Gupta period is called the Golden Age of ancient India. The Chinese pilgrim observes that the king was great patron of art and literature. Chandra Gupta II is credited with maintaining in his court nine lumanaries or great scholars (Nav Ratna). Fa-Hein saw an over 75-metre high image of the Buddha made of copper but it is not traceable now. Beautiful images were made at Mathura and Sarnath, etc.

Rama Gupta

As per recovery of few passages of a lost dramatic work the *Devi Chandra Gupta* by Visakhadatta which has widespread acceptance and its certain references in the *Harshacharita* by Banabhatta, Samudragupta was succeeded by his son Rama Gupta whose wife was Dhruvadevi. While fighting against the Sakas, Rama Gupta was placed in such a difficult position that he agreed to surrender his wife Dhruvadevi to the Saka King. But his younger brother Chandra Gupta II opposed this disgraceful accord, himself went to the Saka camp in the veil of

Dhruvadevi and murdered the Saka King. This incident raised his prestige amongst the people while the reputation of Rama Gupta suffered heavily. Ultimately, Chandra Gupta killed Rama Gupta and succeeded the throne and also married Dhruvadevi. However, there is no historical evidence to prove this story. The contemporary records nowhere mention to Rama Gupta which designate that it was Chandra Gupta II who succeeded his father Samudragupta.

Chandra Gupta II (375 or 380-413 A.D.)

Samudragupta was succeeded by his son, who probably had been associated as *yuvaraja* (crown prince) with his father in the government. He assumed the name of his grandfather according to the Hindu custom, is therefore known as Chandra Gupta II. He also took the title of Vikramaditya, the Sun of Power. He was an able ruler and a great conqueror. He not only extended his father's empire but also consolidated his position through matrimonial alliances with other royal dynasties of the period. He married princess Kuvernaga, daughter of Naga Chieftains and later gave his daughter Prabhavati in marriage to Rudrasena II of powerful family of Vakatakas of the Deccan. This was a great step of diplomacy as it secured the subordinate alliances of the Vakataka king whose territory was of great strategic value in any attack upon the Kshatrapas. Chandra Gupta Vikramaditya ruled from 375 A.D. to 413 A.D. Traditions ascribe to Vikramaditya the foundation of the Vikrama era of 58 B.C.

The Chineses Buddhist pilgrim Fa-Hein (404 A.D.-411 A.D.) visited India during Chandra Gupta II reign. While his stay in India he visited various important places such as Peshawar, Taxila, Mathura, Kapilavastu, Bodh Gaya, Sarnath, Kushinagar and Patliputra. He stayed at Patliputra for three years and has written in detail about the social, political, religious and economic conditions of India in those days. His records are very much reliable and helped a lot in the knowing the history of the Gupta dynasty. Fa-Hein was wonder struck to see the famous royal palace and at Patliputra. His accounts mention that Gupta administration was mild and liberal. The taxes were to be paid by people to the ruler at the rate of 1/4th to 1/6th of the produce. He also mentions that there were trade relations with China, Ceylon and European countries.

His Conquests

An iron pillar inscription at Mehrauli in Delhi indicates that his empire included even north-western India and Bengal. It is a victory pillar which Chandra Gupta Vikramaditya set up after his great victory over the Vahlikas. The greatest military achievement was his victory over the Saka kings, known to European scholars as the Western Kshatrapas who were ruling in western India for centuries. His advance to the Arabian Sea through Malwa and Gujarat, and his subjugation of the peninsula of Saurashtra or Kathiawar is considered to be one of his greatest military successes. With the annexation of Saurashtra and Malwa, he opened up seaports to facilitate trade and commerce. His capital city was Patliputra. In certain records, he has been mentioned as the lord of the city of Ujjain and Patliputra, as he defeated and killed Rudra Sena the last of the great strapas of Ujjain and annexed his dominion. The cool courage he showed in fight with Sakas and killing their king in their own city entitled him the epithets *Sakari* (destroyer of Sakas) or *Sahasanka*. He has also been responsible for the era, popularly known as Vikram Samvat which commence in 58 B.C. This era has been used by major Hindu dynasties and still in use in modern India.

His Character

Chandra Gupta II occupied the throne for nearly forty years, and survived until 413 A.D. His conquest and career prove that he was a strong and vigorous ruler, well qualified to govern an extensive empire. His administration was efficient and enlightened. He loved sounding titles and was fond of depicting himself on his coins as engaged in successful personal combat with a lion. Vikramaditya is also remembered for his patronage of art and literature. He is credited for maintaining *navratna* (nine luminaries) in his court including Kalidasa and Varahmihira. It is, however, uncertain if all of them flourished at the same time. But there is some evidence to show that Kalidas might have been a contemporary of Chandra Gupta II. Kalidas is the greatest Sanskrit poet and dramatist of India. From Fa-Hein's account we come to know that Chandra Gupta II was religiously very tolerant monarch. He made rest-houses for travellers on highways and the capital possessed excellent free hospitals.

Kumara Gupta I (414-55 A.D.)

Chandra Gupta II was succeeded on throne by his son from Queen Dhruva Devi in 414 A.D., who reigned for more than forty years. He is known to history as Kumara Gupta I who assumed the title of "Mahendraditya". He was able to maintain the empire built up by his forefathers, which now extended from north Bengal to Kathiawar and from the Himalayas to the Narbada. The numerous contemporary inscriptions and coins point that during the greater part of his reign the empire witnessed no curtailment. Numismatic evidence even suggests that his influence at one time extended southwards, possibly as far as the Satara district of the Deccan. He even practiced horse-sacrifice as an assertion of his paramount sovereignty and proclaimed himself to be Chakravarti, king of all kings. It is not likely that he would have indulged in this strut unless to some extent justified by successful warfare. During his reign, the whole of India was united as one single entity. Though it was secular and people had their own thoughts and beliefs, yet they remained united and intact in any hardship. Kumar Gupta I was a great patron of art and culture; evidence exist that he endowed a college of fine arts at great ancient university at Nalanda, which flourished during 5th to 12th century A.D. He was a successful ruler who kept intact the vast empire inherited from his father and also maintained peace and prosperity within its frontiers. His period is also regarded as forming part of "the Golden Age" of the Guptas.

Towards the middle of the fifth century A.D., the reign of the Kumara Gupta I was disturbed by the revolt of Pushyamitra tribe, otherwise almost unknown to history, and the invasion of the Hunas of Central Asia. But his greatest achievement was his repulsing the attack of the Pushyamitra. The suppression of Pushyamitras rebellion and the defeat of Hunas by his crown prince prove that the military strength of the empire also remained intact under him. After occupying Bactria the Hunas crossed the Hindukush Mountains and entered India. Their first attack during his reign was repulsed by Prince Skanda Gupta. However, the Guptas could not protect their empire from the Hunas for long and the subsequent waves of Huna invasion made the Gupta's very weak. This was one of the main factors which accelerated the disintegration of the Gupta Empire.

Skanda Gupta (455-67 A.D.)

After the death of Kumara Gupta his son Skanda Gupta ascended the throne in 455 A.D and reigned for twelve years, i.e. 455-67 A.D. He had been engaged in hostilities against his enemies almost from the beginning of his reign. He was an energetic ruler and had saved his father's empire from ruin by attacking back the Pushyamitras. He had defeated the Hunas once as the crown-prince but they were yet threatening the empire with the penetration into the Indian territories. Skanda Gupta courageously fought with them and defeated them so severely about 460 A.D. that they could not dare to attack the empire for nearly fifty years. But, while he was busy in fighting against the Hunas, probably, the Vakatakas ruler Narendrasen occupied Malwa. However, the rest of the territories of empire were kept intact by him.

The Hunas war and possibly other battles which are only vaguely mentioned in official records must have proved a great strain on the financial resources of the empire. This is reflected in the coins of Skanda Gupta. The gold coins issued by him were low in the amount of pure gold. Skanda Gupta has been regarded as the last of the great imperial Guptas. The Empire began to decline after his death and the family could not produce a single ruler who could successfully check this decline. Although petty Gupta kings continued to rule over restricted areas with diminished power. All his successors like Purugupta, Kumar Gupta II, Budhagupta, Bhanugupta, etc. were unable to check the disintegrating forces and the mighty Gupta empire fell before the Hunas.

Administrative System Under the Guptas

The Gupta period marks an important phase in the history of ancient India. The long and efficient rule of the Guptas made a huge impact on the political, social and cultural spheres. Though the Gupta Empire was not as widespread as the Mauryan Empire was in India, yet the Gupta dynasty was successful in creating an empire that is significant in the history of India. In the Mauryan period, the political authority was concentrated in the hands of the king. But the Gupta administration was decentralized in nature. It means that feudatories, i.e. local kings and smaller chiefs ruled a large part of their empire. The vast empire was divided into provinces which were under the control of the governors. The members of the royal family were appointed as governors. Provinces were known as *desha*, *rashtra* or *bhukti* and their head was called *uparika*. The provinces were divided into *vishayas* or *pradesha* or districts. The Mahamatras or provincial viceroys go back to the Mauryan period and continue, in fact, up to the twelfth century as the highest ranks in official bureaucracy. The *gramikas* or the village headmen formed the lowest loop in the ladder. This leaves no doubt about the existence of an organized hierarchy of officials exercising imperial authority in different parts of the country.

The imperial Guptas adopted grandiose titles such as *maharajadhiraja*, *parambhattaraka*, *parameshvara*, etc. The kingship was normally hereditary and the king was the core of administration. Various ministers and princes advised and assisted him. Administrative posts were not only hereditary but often more than one office was combined under the same person. The most important example in this regard was Harisena, the court poet who was the composer of the Allahbad inscription. He has been described as a mahasandhivigrahika (minister of war and peace) as well as mahadandanayaka (chief judicial officer). Initially, these posts were appointed by the king but eventually these became hereditary which might have weakened the administration as the competent persons could not be recruited to responsible posts.

The land tax during Gupta period was known as *bali* which increased considerably. According to Fa-Hein, the land tax was collected at the rate of 1/4th to 1/6th of the produce. The villagers were subjected to forced labour (*vishti*). The Gupta monarchs maintained a standing army. The peasants had to feed the royal army when it passed from the villages. The use of cavalry and horse archery became important in the army. Special attention was paid to the safety of the border areas. The judicial system was elaborated and several law books were written. For the first time civil and criminal laws were differentiated. Disputes connected with various type of property were considered in civil law. Cases related to theft and adultery fell under criminal laws. The king tried cases with the help of the brahmanas. They were easily available to the people. The guilds of merchants and artisans were governed by their own laws. According to Fa-Hein, kings were tolerant, people were prosperous and charitable. People dared not to kill living things.

Gupta Age as the Golden Era

The two hundred years of Gupta rule is undoubtedly the most important in the Indian history from the point of view of literature, science, art, architecture, commerce and colonial developments. The Gupta Period is called the Golden Age of India or the Periclean Age of the classical India. All historians agree that it was the most remarkable period of Indian history when peace and prosperity reigned supreme. The art, literature and religion flowered peacefully. Every aspect of human life, viz. social, political, economic, cultural and religious reached high water marks. The reign of Chandra Gupta I, Samudragupta, Chandra Gupta Vikramaditya, and Kumar Gupta I was undoubtedly the best period in the history of ancient India. Development took place in the field of science, literature, art and architecture and prosperity prevailed in the whole country. The lifestyle and culture of the Gupta dynasty is known through the availability of various ancient coins, scriptures, inscriptions, texts, etc. belonging to that era. Some of the chief achievements of the Gupta period are the following:

1. Growth of Literature: A huge body of religious and secular literature was compiled in this period. The two great epics, the *Ramayana* and the *Mahabharata* were finally completed in the fourth century. The first half of the fourth century also saw the writing of the literature known as Puranas.

The *Vayu Purana*, one of the oldest of the eighteen Puranas, is clearly attributed to this period. Other major Puranas written during this period are the *Vishnu Purana* and the *Matsya Purana*. These texts refer to the stories about the Hindu gods and mention the ways to please them. The *Laws of Manu*, as we now know the book, may be dated from about the beginning of the Gupta period. The literature in Gupta period was written in Sanskrit. The greatest of the poets was Kalidasa who adorned the court of Chandra Gupta II in the fifth century A.D. His most famous literary works are *Malvikagnimitra*, *Abhijnashakuntalam*, *Meghdutam*, *Raghuvamsha*, *Kumarasambhava* and *Ritusambara*. Some of his works are also translated in other important languages of the world. Kalidas's work is undoubtedly occupying a unique position in the Indian history and literature. Another remarkable play, the *Mudra-Rakshasa* of Visakhadatta, tells the story of the usurpation of the crown by Chandra Gupta Maurya, and probably is at least quite as old. *Panchtantra* the renowned book of fables also belongs to this period. Bhairvi, Vasubandoha, Brahagupta and Harisena were great poets of this period.

2. Art and Architecture: The fine art and architecture flourished during this period. They reached the highest point of excellence. Ancient Indian art was greatly influenced by religion. The Sultanganj Buddha image made in copper is most remarkable of the arts. The science of metallurgy reached its zenith. The Iron Pillar at Mehraulli near Qutub Minar is the testimony to the excellence that had been achieved. The pillar has not gathered any rust in the subsequent 15 centuries which exhibit the great technological skill of the time. Beautiful images of Buddha were also created at Mathura and Sarnath. The finest example of Buddhist art during Gupta period are the paintings at Ajanta caves. Ajanta paintings describe the life of Buddha and the colours of these paintings have not faded even after fourteen centuries. The Ajanta caves are now included by the UNESCO in the World Heritage Sites. The Guptas were great patron of music. Samudragupta himself was a great musician and his coins often depict him playing *veena*. The Gupta coins were a great piece of art. These were excellently minted and often portray the activities of its ruler.

Along with the other arts architecture flourished during this period. Vishnu and Shiva cults were gradually replacing Buddhism. It is for the first time that the temples in the form of structures were constructed in north India. These temples were made in Nagara style. Bhitargaon temple in Kanpur and Deogarh temple in Jhansi are best examples of Nagara style architecture during Gupta rule.

3. **Science:** In the field of mathematical and astronomical science, the Gupta age is adorned by the illustrious names of Aryabhata and Varahamihira. Aryabhatta estimated the value of *Pi. Algebra* was developed to a great extent and the concepts of *zero* and *infinity* were found. The symbols of numbers 1 to 9 were devised which was a great contribution in mathematics. These symbols came to be known as Hindu Arabic numerals later when the Arabs too adopted them. Charaka the best physician belonged to this period. As such all round development was made during this period.

4. **Society:** Fa-Hein says that the people led a highly ideal and moral life during the Gupta period. Throughout the whole country, the people do not kill any living being nor drink intoxicating liquor. They do not deal in cattle trade and there were no butcher shops in the market. The people were honest, trustworthy and philanthropists. They had built free hospitals for the poor and the disabled. Special *sarais* (rest houses) had been built on the national highways for the use and benefit of the travelers. However, the structure of society was undergoing a change in the Gupta period. The supremacy of Brahmanas was increasing. They were getting large-scale land grants. There was a great proliferation of castes in this period. The position of women declined in Gupta period. The main reason for the subordination of women was their complete dependence on men for their livelihood. The women were not entitled to inherit property. However, she had full right on her *stridhana*, i.e. the presents received by the bride at the time of her marriage. The free representation of females in paintings and sculptures gives the indication that there was no *purdah* system. However, there is sign of the presence of *sati* (immolation of widow) system. The inscription at Eran (510 A.D.) in Madhya Pradesh gives

clear evidence of *sati*. The position of *shudras* somewhat improved during this period. They could listen to the epics and the puranas and could also perform certain domestic rituals that were earlier banned for them. There is mention of fifteen types of slaves in *Dharmashastras*. They were employed in domestic cleaning and sweeping. Another class emerged in this period, i.e. the untouchables. They were assigned a lower position then the shudras and were engaged in unclean jobs like scavenging and butchery. Fa-Hein mentions that whenever they entered the towns or the market places they would strike a piece of wood to announce their arrival. Still overall the people were highly content and lived a prosperous life.

5. Economy: From Fa-Hein's account it is quite clear that the people were rich and the country was prosperous during the Gupta period. The period was of great agricultural expansion. The facts that contributed to increase in agricultural produce are the use of iron plough share, manure, irrigation, and preservation of cattle wealth. The discovery of large number of gold coins of the period indicates the prosperity of the time. Both inland and foreign trade were greatly flourishing and the wealth of the country was multiplying rapidly. Till 550 A.D. India continued to have trade with the eastern Roman Empire to which it exported silk and spices.

6. Religion: The Gupta period is usually regarded as an era of Brahmanic revival. The conversion of the ancient Brahmanical faith into something like modern Hinduism, its final triumph against Buddhism and Jainism, its spirit of liberalism, its absorption of foreigners within its fold and the practice of tolerance for every religion, are regarded as the distinguishing features of the religious life of the Gupta age. There is no doubt that Brahmanism enjoyed imperial patronage. According to Dr. H.C. Raychaudhuri, "The most noticeable features in the religious life of the people during the Gupta age were the growing importance of Bhakti (loving faith in God) and the love of fellow-beings which found expression in benevolent activities and toleration of the opinions of others".[1]

Decline of Gupta Empire

For nearly 250 years the Gupta Empire provided political unity, good administration, cultural and economic progress to the country. The period has thus been rightly called as the most glorious era in Indian history. Skanda Gupta was the last great king of the Gupta Empire. Even during the later years of Kumar Gupta's reign, the empire was attacked by a tribe called Pushyamitra but it was repulsed, and immediately after the accession of Skanda Gupta, Hunas made inroads, but they too were repelled. Although in the beginning the Gupta king Skanda Gupta tried effectively to stem the march of the Hunas into India, his successors proved to be weak and could not cope with the Huna invaders, who excelled in horsemanship and who possibly used stirrup made of metal. The inscriptions issued by the Hunas show that by 485 A.D. they had occupied eastern Malwa and a large part of central India. Punjab and Rajasthan also passed into their hands. Although the Huna power was soon overthrown by Yasodharman of Malwa and Narasimha Gupta Baladitya of the Gupta dynasty. But this victory over the Hunas could not revive the Gupta Empire.

There were many causes for the downfall of the empire, the chief among them are:

1. Weak Successors: The Gupta Empire was based on the personal character of the monarch. When after Skanda Gupta weak rulers like Puru Gupta, Narsimha Gupta, Kumara Gupta II came to power, they were unable to keep intact such a large empire. There is evidence to show that following the death of Kumara Gupta and Skanda Gupta, there were civil wars and struggles for the throne. For instance, we have the successors of Buddhagupta, highlighting the rule of more than just one king. Those were Vinayagupta in Bengal and Bhanugupta in Iran. They were not only men of weak character but also some of them followed pacifies that affected other spheres of administration, particularly that of military efficiency. In the absence of competent rulers, no empire could be preserved in those times. The Guptas also lost their empire primarily because of their own incompetence.

2. The Foreign Incursion: Foreign invasions were the second major factor in the decline and disappearance of the Guptas. The Huns repeatedly attacked India. No doubt the Gupta rulers defeated them and succeeded in pushing them back. But each successive fight wrecked the zeal of the Gupta power. The resources started depleting. The Huns brought considerable loss and destruction in the economy. The Huna ruler, Toramana conquered an area stretching up to Eran near Bhopal in central India. His son Mihirkula succeeded him in 515 A.D. He is described in texts as a tyrant and an iconoclast. But Huns embraced Hinduism and became an integral part of Indian society.

3. Uprising of Pushyamitras: The Pushyamitra tried to break away from the Gupta Empire in the time of Kumar Gupta I but Skand Gupta defeated them. But the repeated conflicts had sapped the enthusiasm of the Gupta army. Taking advantage of the weakness of the central power the provincial governors started to assert their independence. The Gupta Empire was divided into small kingdoms with no strong central authority to keep it under control.

4. Rise of Yasodharman: The ambitious Chief Yasodharman man established his independent kingdom. The independence declared by Yasodharman of Malwa dealt a server blow to the Gupta Empire. He became very strong and started defying the Gupta power. The Malwa prince successfully challenged the authority of the Guptas and set up pillars of victory commemorating his conquest (532 A.D.) of almost the whole of northern India. Indeed Yasodharman's rule was short-lived, but he dealt a severe blow to the Gupta Empire.

5. Economic Reasons: The collapse of the Gupta Empire can never be explained without a reference to the economic decline. The continuous wars depleted the royal treasury and it became extremely difficult for them to carry on the day-to-day administrative expenses of the empire. Another economic reason was decrease in country's trade and commerce. Till 550 A.D. India had good trade relations with Roman Empire to which it exported silk and spices. But as the Romans learnt the art of rearing silk worms, it greatly affected the trade relations between the two empires. The loss in trade lessened the inflow of gold and silver into the country. It is confirmed by a general scarcity of gold coins in the later Gupta period and the available coins also had less of gold and more of alloy. The revenue income of the government was considerably reduced under the later Gupta rulers as a result of the large-scale land grants made by the Gupta emperors.

6. Internal Dissensions: The Gupta monarchs did not follow any definite law of succession and after the death of almost every monarch there was a war of succession. In fact, after Kumara Gupta the succession to the throne was always disputed. Probably, even Skanda Gupta had to fight against Pura Gupta to get the throne. And after Skanda Gupta, his step-brother Puru Gupta had to fight against Kumara Gupta II, son of Skanda Gupta to get the throne. The family quarrels greatly undermined the prestige of the Guptas and ultimately led to the downfall of their empire. Their court had become the pivot of intrigues under the weak successors with the result that it hastened the downfall of the glorious dynasty of the Guptas.

7. Weakness of Army: The Gupta period was a long period of peace and prosperity. The peaceful atmosphere not only made the people very ease loving but also affected adversely the martial spirit of the soldiers. They became easy going and when they had to fight against powerful enemies like Huns they proved incompetent and incapable and suffered heavy losses. It has been rightly remarked, "An empire with such a weak military had no alternate but to go to the wall."

8. The Vastness of the Empire: The Gupta Empire was very wide in range and it was hence very difficult to control such a stretched-out empire by an incompetent ruler. The means of communication were very primitive and had not developed so much. If there was any revolt in the distant province like Bengal, Gujarat, the rebellious chief could not become an independent ruler before the arrival of the royal forces. This vastness of the empire was a dominant factor which sealed the fall of the Gupta Empire.

Hence, show up the downfall of a mighty empire whose rule had been known as the Golden Age of ancient India. It is well said that the decline of the Gupta Empire was brought about by the same causes which operated in the case of the Mauryan Empire in the earlier times and the Mughals in the later days. The decline of the Guptas led to the emergence of numerous ruling dynasties in northern India. The prominent among them were the Pushyabhutis of Thanesar, Maukharins of Kanauj and the Maitrakas of Valabhi. The political scene in the Peninsular India was no different. The Chalukyas and the Pallavas emerged as strong regional powers in Deccan and the northern Tamil Nadu respectively.

The Huns

The Huns were a group of nomadic herdsmen, war-like people from the steppes of North Central Asia north of China who terrorized, pillaged, and destroyed much of Asia and Europe from the 3rd through 5th centuries. The use of the stirrup gave the Huns a technological advantage over other warriors of the time. Stirrups are loops hung from a saddle that support a horse rider's feet; these let the Huns brace themselves on their horses while wielding swords or shooting arrows. The Huns divided into two main streams, one directed towards the valley of the Volga, and the other to that of the Oxus valley. The former poured into Eastern Europe in 375 A.D., forcing the Goths to the south of the Danube, and the later settled down upon Persia and India in the fifth century A.D. They were known as White Huns. Another nomadic tribe Yueh-chi was forced to migrate from their neighbourhood because of their pressure which ultimately led to the invasion of the Sakas and the Kushanas on India. The inroads of Huns into India began in the reign of Kumara Gupta, under Toramana. The early incursion of Huns into India was repulsed by Skanda Gupta as crown prince, but they renewed their attacks when the great emperor was no more. Toramana is known to have been established as a ruler of Malwa in central India prior to 500 A.D. He died in about 510 A.D., and the empire he consolidated in India passed on to his son Mihirkula, whose capital in India was Sakala, modern Sialkot, in the Punjab. Mihirkula was once defeated and was forced to bow before Yasodharman of Malwa. Therefore, his empire remained limited to Kashmir, Gandhara and certain other territories west of the *R*. Indus.

V.A. Smith characterises the Hun invasion as a "turning point in the history of northern India both political and social". The Hun invasions broke up the political system of the Guptas and destroyed the political unity of India. The result was that many new kingdoms sprang into existence. The chief among them being the Maitrakas of Vallabhi, the Maukharis of Kannauj, the Gurjaras of Rajputana, the Gaudas of Bengal and the later Guptas of Malwa and Magadha and the Pushyabhutis of Thaneswar though, of course, Yasodharman also established a powerful kingdom for himself in Malwa for some time. However, around 567 A.D., the central power of the Huns on the Oxus was broken by the combined forces of the Turks and the Persians. The Huns hence remained not in a position to threaten India and were finally absorbed within the Indian society.

Yasodharman

Yasodharman probably belonged to Aulikara family whose members ruled in Malwa, central India since 4th century A.D. Nothing is known about the predecessors of Yasodharman. He faced the anarchy in Malwa which was brought by the incursions of the Hunas and the frequent attacks of the Vakatakas, and declared himself the ruler of Malwa in 530 A.D. He was a Saiva ruler who has left records of his achievements on a Pillar at Mandsaur. He is described as the king who subdued even those regions which the imperial Guptas and the Huns were unable to conquer. His court poet inscribed that Yasodharman mastered northern India from the Brahmaputra to the Western Ocean and from the Himalaya to Mount Mahendra, which probably should be understood to mean the southernmost peak (Mahendragiri) of the Travancore Ghats. But the silence of Hiuen Tsang suggests that Yasodharman made the most of his achievements, and that his court poet gave him something more than his due of praise. The Hun ruler Mihirkula, whose head had never been bowed in humiliation to any mortal, was urged to do reverence to Yasodharman's feet.

IMPORTANT QUESTIONS

1. What are the sources for studying the history of the Imperial Guptas?
2. How do coins and inscriptions throw light on the personality and achievements of Samudra Gupta? Is it correct to describe him as Indian Napoleon?
3. Give an account of the Gupta administration. How far did it differ from that of the Mauryas?
4. Examine the progress in the fields of art and religion in India during 300 A.D.–550 A.D.
5. Evaluate the new trends which emerged in society and economy during the period from 300 A.D.–550 A.D.
6. Discuss the causes of the downfall of the Gupta Empire.
7. "The Gupta Age was the Golden Age of ancient Indian history." Comment.

NOTE

1. H.C. Raychaudhuri, *An Advanced History of India*, p. 192.

REFERENCES

Basham, A.L., *The Wonder That Was India,* Delhi: Surjeet Publications, 2007.

Chaurasia, R.S., *History of Ancient India* (*Earliest times to 1200 A.D.*), New Delhi: Atlantic Publishers, 2008.

Encyclopedia Britannica.

E notes, National Institute of Open Learning.

Raychaudhuri, *An Advanced History of India*, New Delhi: Macmillan Publishers, 1978.

Sharma, L.P., *History of Ancient India* (*Pre-historic Age to 1200 A.D.*), New Delhi: Konark Publishers.

Smith, Vincent A., *The Early History of India*, New Delhi: Atlantic Publishers, 1999.

Successors of the Guptas (550 A.D.–750 A.D.)

12

Maitrakas of Vallabhi

The Maitrakas established themselves as independent rulers in Saurashtra (Kathiawar) from the 5th to the 8th century A.D. (i.e. nearly 300 years). Taking advantage of the decline of Guptas a chief named Bhatarka of Maitraka clan established a dynasty at Saurashtra with Vallabhi as its capital. They were loose feudatory to the Guptas but still independent in rule. The earlier kings of Vallabhi do not appear to have been independent, and were doubtless obliged to pay tribute to the Huns; but after the destruction of the Hun domination, the lords of Vallabhi asserted their independence, and made themselves a considerable power in the west of India, both on the mainland and in the peninsula of Saurashtra. The kingdom became very influential under Shiladitya I, who was a Buddhist. He conquered regions of Malwa and Rajasthan. His nephew Dhruvasena II was the most important ruler of the Maitrakas. He was Harsha's son-in-law. Later, however, the Maitrakas suffered at the hands of the Chalukyas of the Deccan and Harshavardhana of Kannauj. Vallabhi during the close of the seventh century grew up as a great centre of learning. Hiuen Tsang says the city was famous in Buddhist church history as having been the residence of two distinguished teachers, Gunamati and Sthiramati, in the sixth century. I-tsing, a junior contemporary of Hiuen Tsang, tells us that in his time Nalanda in South Bihar and Vallabhi were two places in India which deserved comparison with the most famous centres of learning in China, and were frequented by crowds of eager students, who commonly devoted two or three years to attendance at lectures on Buddhist philosophy. Being on the Arabian Sea, it was also a port town having flourishing trade and commerce. The rulers of this dynasty were great patron of religious foundation. According to tradition, it was in Vallabhi that the Shvetambara Jaina canon was codified. After Harsha's death the Maitrakas revived, although the kingdom was probably overthrown by the Arabs of Sindh until about 770 A.D.

Maukharis of Kannauj

The Maukharis were originally feudatories of the Guptas, although they established their independence at Kannauj in the 6th century. The dynasty's founder, Ishanavarman, ruled under the title *Maharajadhiraja*. He was the most powerful of the Maukharis king, who successfully fought against the Andhras, the Sulikas and the Gaudas. He was succeeded by Sarvavarman, Avantivarman, and Grihavarman. Nothing of importance is known either of Sharvavarman or of Avantivarman. Grihavarman was married to the daughter of Prabhakarvardhana of the Pushyabhuti family of Thanesar and sister of Rajyavardhana and Harshavardhan. Shashanka, the ruler of Bengal (Gaur) and Dev Gupta, the later Gupta ruler jointly attacked Grihavarman and killed him. The kingdom of Kannauj was then merged with that of the Pushyabhutis of Thanesar and Harsha shifted his capital from Thanesar (Kurukshetra) to Kannauj. The importance of the history of the Maukharis lies in the fact that they offered the most stubborn opposition to the Huns.

Vakatakas (Peninsular India)

After the disintegration of the Satavahana dynasty several small kingdoms grew up in the different provinces, which were previously under them. The Abhiras usurped the provinces of Gujarat, Konkan and Northern Maharashtra including the districts of Nasik and Khandesh. The Ikshvakus became the rulers in the Andhra region. South Kosal and Kalinga were probably divided into small chiefdoms. Vidarbha and southern Konkan were overrun by the Vakatakas.

The Vakatakas were a local power that ruled over northern Maharashtra and Vidarbha. Their history can be reconstructed on the support of a large number of land grant charters issued to the brahmanas. Vakataka dynasty, originating in the central Deccan in the mid-3rd century A.D., the empire of which is believed to have extended from Malwa and Gujarat in the north to the Tungabhadra in the south and from the Arabian Sea in the west to the Bay of Bengal in the east. The Vakatakas, like many of the contemporary dynasties of the Deccan, claimed Brahmanical origin. Little is known, however, about Vindhyashakti (*c.* 250-70 A.D.), the founder of the family. Territorial expansion began in the reign of his son Pravarasena I, who came to the throne about 270 A.D. and reached the R. Narmada in the north by annexing the kingdom of Purika. Pravarasena's kingdom was partitioned after his death. The main line continued with Rudrasena I (330 A.D.), his son Prithvisena I (350 A.D.), and Prithvisena's son Rudrasena II (400 A.D.). Because of its territorial position, the Vakataka family was recognized as a useful ally of Guptas. Rudrasena II was married to Prabhavati Gupta, the daughter of Chandra Gupta II. In this period, Gupta impact was significant in Vakataka polity and culture. Rudrasena's death was followed by the lengthy dominance of Prabhavati Gupta during the minority of her sons Divakarasena and Damodarasena.

After the Guptas became involved in a war against the Hunas, the Vakataka dynasty was free to expand in central India. Vakataka influence spread to such central Indian states as Kosala, Mekala, and Malava. Prithvisena II was the last known king of the line, who acceded to the throne about 470. Culturally, the Vakataka kingdom is important because it became a channel to spread brahmanical culture to south India. The rulers of this dynasty patronized both Sanskrit and Prakrit languages. Most of them were themselves scholars. King Pravarasena wrote the *Setu-Bandh* and king Sarvasena wrote the *Hari-Vijaya*. Both are in poetic form and the language is Prakrit. The paintings of cave numbers 16 and 17 of Ajanta were also prepared during their rule.

Pushyabhutis of Thanesar

The Pushyabhutis played a far more influential and distinguished role than any other dynasty which rose to power after the fall of the Imperial Guptas. They had their capital at Thanesar (in modern Kurukshetra). The rulers of Thanesar were feudatory chiefs of the Maukharis but ultimately succeeded in asserting their independence. According to *Harshacharita* of Banabhatta, the first independent ruler of this dynasty was Pushyabhuti, a devoted worshipper of *Siva*. The third ruler Aditya Vardhana married the sister of Mahasena Gupta, one of the later Gupta rulers. His son and successor was Prabhakara Vardhan who assumed the title of *Maharajadhiraja*. The empire became influential under him as he was able to defeat the Malavas, the Huns, and the Gujaras, probably those of Rajputana and strengthen his position in the regions of Punjab and Haryana. So great was his power that Grihavarman of Maukhari dynasty courted his alliance by marrying his daughter Rajyasri. After his death, his elder son Rajya Vardhana came to the throne but he was unscrupulously killed by Sashanka, king of central Bengal. Sashanka entered into an alliance with Deva Gupta, ruler of Malwa who was the enemy of the ruler of Thanesar. Deva Gupta attacked Kannauj and Sashanka helped him just after the death of Prabhakara Vardhana, killed Grihavarman and made Rajyasri, wife of Grihavarman and sister of Rajya Vardhana, the then ruler of Thanesar, a captive.

Harsha Vardhana (606-647 A.D.)

On the tragic murder of his brother, Harsha Vardhana ascended the throne in 606 A.D. He was the last great ruler of ancient India. He was the younger son of Prabhakar Vardhana and ascended the throne only at the age of sixteen years. Initially, he was scrupled to express his consent and consulted a Buddhist oracle before accepting the invitation. Both Bana and Hiuen Tsang refer to Harsha's reluctance to mount the throne. Still he proved himself worthy of the trust reposed in him and acted like a great warrior and an able administrator. He commemorated his accession by founding a new era known as the Harsha era. The first task before Harsha after ascending the throne was to avenge the murder of his brother and rescue his widowed sister Rajyasri, whose husband had been treacherously murdered by Deva Gupta, the ruler of Malwa. Harsha was informed that his widowed sister had escaped from confinement, and fled to the Vindhyan forests in disgust. He first tried to trace her and succeeded in doing so that moment she was going to throw herself into fire. Harsha Vardhan then amalgamated his kingdom with that of his widowed sister Rajyasri and then transferred his capital from Thanesar to Kannauj. Though we have the inscription at Nalanda and Banskhera and coins of that age, yet two valuable sources that throw important light on the life and times of Harsha Vardhana are *Harshacharita* written by his court poet Banabhatta and *Si-Yu-Ki*, the travel account of the Chinese Buddhist pilgrim Hiuen Tsang, who visited India during 629-44 A.D.

His Conquests

Harsha having recovered his sister devoted his ability and energy to the prosecution of a methodical scheme of conquest, with the deliberate purpose of bringing all India 'under one umbrella'. He possessed at this stage of his career a force of 5,000 elephants, 20,000 cavalry, and 50,000 infantry. With this mobile and formidable force, Harsha overran northern India; and, in the picturesque language of his contemporary the Chinese pilgrim, "he went from east to west subduing all who were not obedient". By the end of five and a half years, the conquest of the north-western regions, and probably also of a large portion of Bengal, was completed; and his military resources were so increased that he was able to put in the field 60,000 war elephants and 100,000 cavalry. He then reigned happily for thirty-five years longer, and during that period devoted most of his immense energy to the government of his extensive dominions. His last recorded campaign, an attack on the sturdy inhabitants of Ganjam, on the coast of the Bay of Bengal, took place in 643 A.D. Following were his important wars for conquests:

1. War against Sashanka of Bengal: Harsha had to avenge the death of his elder brother who was treacherously killed by Sashanka, the ruler of Bengal. He collected his large army and entered into an alliance with Bhaskara Varman, the ambitious king of Kamarupa in modern Assam. Another prince befriended by Harsha was Madhava Gupta, belonging to the line of the "later Guptas" of Malwa and Magadha. While Harsha was busy in recovering his sister, Bhand was ordered to proceed against the kings of Gauda. The details of the campaign against Sashanka of Gauda have not been recorded, and it seems clear that he escaped with little loss. He was a formidable opponent and his power seems to have continued undiminished till 619 A.D. His kingdom probably became subject to Harsha at a later date.

2. Conquest of Five Indies: According to the Chinese pilgrim, Hiuen Tsang, Harsha had spent about six years of his early reign, i.e. from 606 A.D. to 612 A.D. in persistent warfare until he had fought the 'Five Indies'. These include eastern Punjab, Kannauj, Bengal, Bihar and Orissa and subduing many other states both in the east and the west.

3. War against Pulakesin II: Harsha's long career of victory was broken by one failure. He in 620 A.D. turned his attention towards the Deccan. But there he received a check at the hand of the greatest of the Chalukya ruler Pulakesin II. He competed with Harsha in the extent of his conquests, and had raised himself to the rank of lord paramount of the South, as Harsha was of the North. The northern king, who could not willingly endure the existence of so powerful a rival, ventured to overthrow him, advancing in person to the attack, with 'troops from the five Indies and the best generals from all countries'. But the effort failed. The king of the Deccan guarded the passes on the Narmada so effectually that Harsha was constrained to retire defeated, and to accept that river as his frontier.

4. Conquest of Vallabhi (Gujarat): Vallabhi or modern Gujarat was then ruled by a powerful ruler Dhruvasena (Dhruvabhata) II. Harsha could not tolerate the existence of a powerful monarchy on the borders of his empire. So he attacked Vallabhi and defeated its ruler. But due to the intervention of Dadda II of Baroach, Harsha patched up his differences with Dhruvasena II by marrying his daughter. The latter was reinstated in his kingdom but now he began to rule Vallabhi as a feudatory prince under Harsha.

5. Conquest of Ganjam: Harsha's last conquest was that of Ganjam, which was a small state on the eastern coast of India. In the beginning because of the rivalry of Sashanka he could not get much success but after his death in 642 A.D. Harsha conquered the territory in 643 A.D.

6. Relations with Nepal, Sind and Kashmir: There occurred certain border disputes between Harsha and the rulers of Sindh, Kashmir and Nepal but these kingdoms remained independent of the influence of Harsha. However, it is not certain and there is a great controversy among scholars whether these kingdoms acknowledged Harsha's superiority or not.

Administration under Harsha

Harsha governed his empire very much like the Guptas. He himself was the head of the state, and all legislative, administrative and judicial powers were settled in his hands. He was also the first Commander-in-Chief of his army. Detailed administration of course remained in the hands of the local Rajas, but the orders of the suzerain were obeyed. For the control of his extensive empire, Harsha relied upon his personal supervision, exercised with untiring energy, rather than upon the services of a trained bureaucracy. The principal source of state income was land revenue called *bhaga* amounting to 1/6th of the produce. Harsha divided the country into a number of provinces (*bhuktis*) and appointed a Viceroy (*Uparika*) for each of the provinces. The viceroys with the help of ministers and other officers ruled the country. The provinces were further subdivided into districts (*vishayas*) and officials (*Vishayapati*) were appointed to look after the affairs of the districts. The village was the smallest unit of administration. The principal officer of a village was *Gramika*. Records were properly maintained. The officials looked after the material and moral characters of the people. These officials were awarded by land grants (*jagirs*). Thus, feudalism (jagirdari system) was further given impetus during the reign of Harsha. Charitable institutions were set up all over the country. He took many useful public welfare steps and tried to maintain peace and order by strict punishment to offenders. But his law and order was not that well maintained as compared to the Guptas. Violent crime was rare, but the roads and river routes evidently were less safe than in Fa-Hein's time, as Hiuen Tsang was robbed more than once.

Harsha had maintained a large standing army. According to Hiuen Tsang, the army of Harsha constituted 60,000 war elephants and 1,00,000 cavalry.

Socio-economic Condition

The people were well off and there were families with great wealth. They led a just and humble life. They avoided the consumption of meat and liquor. Their attire was simple yet glossy and use of silk was common. However, there were rigid caste restrictions and untouchability was in vogue. There was no *Purdah system* but there were several restrictions on the free movements of women in the society. The practice of sati was getting encouragement, though only restricted to higher section of the society. Reference to this was in the *Harshacharita* of Bana, the queen performs *sati* on the death of her husband king Prabhakara Vardhana. Even Rajyasri, sister of Harsha was about to perform *sati* when Harsha rescued her. Both internal and external trade flourished. Gold and silver coins were in use. Kannauj, the imperial capital of Harsha was an extensive, prosperous and well-protected city. There were beautiful gardens and tanks of clear water. It was resided by highly learned, cultured and rich people. The people, in general, were interested in literary and fine art learning. Since Harsha Vardhana was a staunch Buddhist, non-violence was the order of the day.

Religious Conditions

Hinduism, Jainism and Buddhism were still the popular religions of India. The members of the Royal family to which Harsha belonged freely acted on their individual preferences in the matter of religion. Pushyabhuti was a devotee of Siva and Harsha's father was worshipper of the Sun. Harsha himself was the worshipper of Siva and the Sun and followed Hinduism in his early life. Later when he came in contact with Hiuen Tsang, the Chinese Law Master, he started showing a strong inclination for Buddhism. Though he did not completely abandon the Saivism of his earlier years, he employed all his state machinery for the spread of Buddhism. He established benevolent institutions throughout the empire on the Asokan model, for the benefit of travellers, the poor, and sick. He erected rest-houses and monasteries and practised charity on an extensive scale. He forbade the slaughter of any living being or the use of flesh as food throughout the 'Five Indies'. The king also imitated his prototype in the foundation of numerous religious establishments, devoted to the service of both the Hindu gods and the Buddhist ritual. In his closing years, the latter received the chief share of the royal favour; and numerous monasteries were erected, as well as several thousand stupas, each about 100 feet high, built along the banks of the sacred Ganges. Harsha also began to call the annual meetings of the Buddhist Sangha. He even called an assembly at Kannauj in honour of the Chinese pilgrim Hiuen Tsang. Buddhist monks were given special grants of land and money. But Harsha was never a convert to Buddhism and continued to worship Siva and Surya even during the later period of his life. Thus, he practised a policy of religious toleration.

Education and Literature

Education was widely diffused, especially among the Brahmanas and numerous Buddhist monks; and learning was honoured by the government. According to V.A. Smith, "Harsha was not only a liberal patron of literary merit, but was himself an accomplished calligraphist and an author of reputation."[1] He was considered to be a literary monarch who has written three plays: *Priyadarshika* or *Gracious Lady*, *Nagananda* and *Ratnavali* or *Necklace*. As Sanskrit was the popular language of the time so all these plays were written in Sanskrit. Harsha was also a great patron of learning and scholars. It has been said that he spent one-fourth of his income on education and learning. Amongst the greatest scholars whom he patronized the name of Banabhatta stands distinct. He was the court poet of Harsh who wrote *Harshacharita* praising his patron. Written in an ornate style, it became a model for later writers. The early history of Harsha is reconstructed on the basis of this text. Another text written by him is *Kadambari*. He also patronized the Chinese traveller Hiuen Tsang who wrote *Si-Yu-Ki*. Divakara and Jayasena were also present at Harsha's court. The universities of Nalanda, Vallabhi and the one run by Divakara in Vindhya forest were great centres of learning at that time.

Achievements of Harsha

1. A Great Conquerer: He was a great conquerer who brought order out of chaos. He conquered petty battling states. He waged continuous and ruthless wars and became the undisputed master of Northern India. He united Thanesar and Kannauj, waged wars against Sasank of Bengal. Devagupta of Malwa, conquered Five Indies—Punjab, Kanauj, Orissa, Bengal, Bihar. He also conquered Gujarat.

2. An Able Ruler: Harsha was a great and efficient administrator. He did not oppress his people. There was no forced labour, taxes were light, and crimes were rare. He personally looked after the whole administration. The Chinese pilgrim remarks: "the day was too short for him. He was the busiest of men and devoted all his time to promote the welfare of his people."

3. A Great Empire Builder: He not only won new territories but also gave a good administration to the country he conquered. After the collapse of the Gupta Empire not only the unity of the country was broken but all the administrative machinery of the country had gone to the winds. He gave the country the long desired unity and efficient, systematised administration.

4. A Great Religious Leader: In the words of Dr. Raychaudhuri, "A great general and a just administrator, he (Harsha) was even greater as a patron of religion and learning."[2] He employed all his state machinery for the service of Buddhism. He never behaved like a religious begot. He never persecuted others for the sake of his personal religion.

5. A Great Scholar and Patron of Learning: According to Dr. Raychaudhuri, "Harsha showed a taste for literature and the arts of peace that reminds one of the versatile hero, Samudragupta." He composed three Sanskrit Dramas—the *Ratnavali*, the *Priyadarsika* and the *Nagananda*. All three are still available and testify the great literary attainments of the royal author. He was a great patron of literature and education. He extended liberal patronage to the great scholars of the day. Bana Bhatta the great court poet wrote *Harshacharita* and the *Kadambri*. The other scholars at his court were Malanga, Diwakar, Jaysena and Bhartri Hari, etc.

An Estimate of Harsha

He was a strong and vigorous ruler, relentless in the discharge of his public duties. He combined in himself some of the characteristic attributes of both Samudragupta and Asoka. His thorough going conquests in different directions recall the military career of Samudragupta. When his wars were over, he, like Asoka, devoted himself to the task of peace, the promotion of the moral and material progress.

Successors of Harsha Vardhana

Hiuen Tsang gives the information that King Harsha died either in 646 A.D. or the beginning of 647 A.D., not long after his distinguished guest's departure. Emperor Harsha left no successor to his throne. His empire was divided amongst his nobles and provincial governors which brought about the destruction of the Vardhana Empire.

Hiuen Tsang

Hiuen Tsang was the most celebrated of all the Chinese pilgrims who came to India. He visited India in the first half of the seventh century A.D. and spent about 15 years (630-45 A.D.). During this period, he travelled all over the country and observed everything very minutely. He came to this country with the chief aim of collecting the Buddhist scriptures and visited all those places connected with the Sakyamuni but his sharp eyes left nothing unnoticed. He returned to his country with a lot of material connected with the Buddhist faith—relics, images and about 657 volumes of manuscripts. He has put down all his experiences and observations in a book entitled *Si-Yu-Ki* or the records of the Western world. This book is an invaluable source of information about the condition of the country as well as the religion, manners and customs of the time. He became a personal friend of king Harsha and spent about eight years in his dominion. He returned home by the southern route crossing the Pamirs and travelling through Khotan. His account of the state of the country under Harsha is as follows:

Harsha's Administration: Hiuen Tsang was favourably impressed by the administrative arrangements of king Harsha. The king wanted to have a first-hand knowledge of the condition of the people committed to his charge. So he frequently undertook tours of inspection and governed his vast empire by incessant personal supervision. It was only in the rainy season that his tours were suspended. The government was thus personal and not bureaucratic like that of the Mauryas. The king was probably assisted by a council of ministers "Mantri Parishad". It was such a council headed by Bhandi, the chief minister of his deceased brother that had called him to the throne. The official hierarchy was the same as that at the time of the Guptas. The outlying provinces were governed by local chiefs who owed allegiance to the imperial throne.

Taxation and Revenue: The administration was conducted on benign principles. Taxation was light. The revenue was derived from crown lands and was assessed as one-sixth of the produce. Forced labour on public works was paid for. Officials were remunerated by grants of land made according to their work and position. The Chinese pilgrim emphasises that the families were not registered. The enlightened character of the administration is shown in the creation of a department of records. There were special officers in each province who kept official records of all public events whether good or bad. The government interested itself most actively in the higher life as well as in the material comforts of the community.

Benevolent Institutions: Benevolent institutions for the benefit of travellers, the poor and the sick were established throughout the empire and liberal provision was made for charity to various religious communities. Education was widely diffused and learning was honored by the government. Harsha was a patron of learners and was himself an accomplished scholar and the reputed author of their Sanskrit dramas of high merit. The Buddhist monasteries at Nalanda and other places were centres of learning and art.

Social and Economic Conditions: The people wore simple dress comprising inner clothing and outward garment which did not involve any tailoring work. They were very fond of ornaments. Most of the people went barefooted and shoes were rare. The food of the people was very simple and pure. They generally took milk, ghee, rice, gram and vegetables, etc.

Onions and garlics were very rarely used and the use of meat was not so common. About the architecture and house planning Hiuen Tsang writes that their walls were generally built of bricks and often coated with chunam. The roofs were sometimes made of thatched reed matting but generally there were wooden flat roofed rooms which were often covered with tiles burnt or unburnt. The floors were purified with cowdung and stretch with flowers of the season. Their houses on short were "sumptuous inside and economical outside and impressive".

State of Education and Religion: Harsha was a patron of learning and was himself an accomplished scholar. Buddhism was still strong, although Hinduism was gaining way. Harsha formed all the religious doing honour in turn to Shiva, the Sun and Buddha. In the later part of his reign, he became more and more Buddhist in sentiment. There seems to have been considerable ill-feeling between the various sects, although there was no general religious persecution. But there was one exception. Sasanka king of Bengal persecuted the Buddhist and is said to have destroyed the Bodh tree of Gaya and to have broken to pieces the stone masked with the footprints of Lord Buddha but it seems heresy.

Harsha and His Assemblies: Hiuen Tsang has given a vivid description of Harsha's Assemblies. Harsha called a special Assembly at Kannauj to honour Hiuen Tsang and to give wide publicity to the doctrine of Mahayana faith. In this Assembly very heated discussion took place between the Brahmans and Hiuen Tsang. In the end Hiuen Tsang won the day and a special procession was organised to honour him on his success, Harsha also held assemblies at Prayag where he used to distribute alms among the learned religious men, the poor and the needy on a very large scale. One of such assemblies was held in 643 A.D. which was attended by Harsha himself. On the first day Harsha worshipped Buddha, on the second day the image of Sun and on the third day adoration was offered to Shiva. He then distributed wealth and offered gifts to people of creed and sects who were needy and poor and destitutes. He also presented rich gifts to Brahmans and Buddhist monks and learned men.

Thus, we find Hiuen Tsang's account about Harsha's court and life in those days is far vivid and detailed than that of Fa-Hein's about Guptas' period.

NALANDA AND VALLABHI UNIVERSITIES

Nalanda University

Nalanda was the famous centre of higher education where students flocked from far and wide. It counted 10,000 students on its rolls. The university provided not only free education but also free board and lodging. The revenues of one hundred villages were remitted for its endowment. The university was meant for advanced studies and so the administration was strict. Its foundation stone was laid by Kumar Gupta I in the middle of fifth century. It was situated on Bihar about 13 km from the historical city of Rajgriha. In the beginning, it was a simple monastery but soon it developed into the most renowned seat of learning and literary activities for imparting higher education to the students. They had organised many advanced centres of learning which resembled more or less the modern universities. Some of the famous ancient universities were those of Taxila, Ujjain, Kashi, Kanchi, Panchal, Vikramshila but the most important of these universities was the Nalanda University. It is rightly described as "The Oxford of Mahayana Buddhism". It followed a wide curriculum of studies and day by day it rose to prominence and became an international seat of learning. Students came here from China, Tibet, Central Asia, Bukhara, Korea, Java and other places. The teachers of Nalanda used to be most renowned scholars of other particular subjects. The names of Dharampal, Chandrapal, Shilbhatta, Dharam Kerti, Gunamati, Sitharmati, Padam Sambhava who taught and guided the students in various subjects are still famous all over the world for their deep knowledge and learning. Hiuen Tsang was the student of Nalanda University for over five years. Another Chinese student was I-tsing. The rulers of India gave their patronage to this university and by their lavish grants, gifts and endowments they greatly contributed to its popularity. During Harsha's time as many as 10,000 students were studying in the university and as many as 1510 teachers were busy imparting knowledge to the students. Harsha also built a monastery there which was about 100 feet in height and was covered with brass plates. Indians as well as some foreign rulers thought it to be their good fortune if they were allowed to add something to this university. "Kings vied with one another on their liberality to equip and endow this great institution." Nalanda thus had huge monastic establishment in the time of Harshvardhana. The university specialised in the study of Mahayana doctrines but its curriculum included the study of the literature of other Buddhist sects as well as Brahmanical literature both sacred and secular. Scholars came there to put an end to their doubts and learn. The admission to the university was very difficult. Those who were fortunate enough to get admission were provided free board and lodging. There were separate arrangements for hostel facilities.

According to Hiuen Tsang, there was cordial relation between the teachers and the taught. The Nalanda University had a long line of distinguished professors. Shilbhadra was the head of the Nalanda University. He was a friend and teacher of Hiuen Tsang. The teachers were held in high respects and were looked up to as models all over India. According to Hiuen Tsang, "The students of this university were nothing less than ideal students and since the establishment of the monastery there was not a single case of breach of the discipline."

The course of studies comprised all the works of the eighteen schools of Buddhism and also included such varied subjects as the Vedas, Astronomy, Medicine, Sciences, Logic, Grammar and Philosophy in its curriculum. Nalanda was much responsible for spreading Indian culture in many foreign countries like Tibet, China and Central Asia. In the words of Dr. Tripathi, we can conclude that, "Its lofty structure its inspiring instructions imparted through discussion, its comprehensive curriculum, its large assemblage of students from far and near, and above all, the noble character and deep scholarships of its teachers and alumni were then matters of pride to the entire Buddhist world."

Nalanda continued to flourish in India for many centuries till it was destroyed towards the end of 12th century by Muhammad Bin Bakhtiyar Khilji one of the lieutenants of

Mohd. Ghori. Its library and buildings were set on fire and thus vanished the great sects of ancient Indian learning and culture under the hammer of its brute invader.

Vallabhi

The University of Vallabhi was in Kathiawar (Gujarat). It was considered to be a great centre of learning and culture in the seventh century. The education imparted there was of no fewer standards than that of Nalanda. Students flocked here to get higher education from all parts of India and abroad. The Mayatric rulers of Saurashtra had endowed this seat of learning. It had specialised in the 'Thervad School of Buddhism'. There was also a big library attached to this university. During Harsha's rule there was peace and prosperity and progress in all spheres of life.

IMPORTANT QUESTIONS

1. Give a short history of the Vakatakas during the period of your study.
2. Describe the life and achievements of Harsha Vardhana.
3. "Harsha was the last empire builder of ancient India." How far do you agree with this view?
4. Give an estimate of Hiuen Tsang's description of India during the period of Harsha Vardhana.
5. Write a short note on the Nalanda University.

NOTES

1. V.A. Smith, *The Early History of India*, p. 342.
2. H.C. Raychaudhuri, *An Advanced History of India*, p. 153.

REFERENCES

Basham, A.L., *The Wonder That Was India*, Delhi: Surjeet Publishers, 2007.

Chaurasia, R.S., *History of Ancient India* (*Earliest times to 1200 A.D.*), New Delhi: Atlantic Publishers, 2008.

Encyclopedia Britannica.

E notes, National Institute of Open Learning.

Raychaudhuri, *An Advanced History of India*, New Delhi: Macmillan Publishers, 1978.

Sharma, L.P., *History of Ancient India* (*Pre-historic Age to 1200 A.D.*), New Delhi: Konark Publishers, 1996.

Smith, V.A., *The Early History of India*, New Delhi: Atlantic Publishers, 1999.

Post Harsha North India
(647 A.D.–1200 A.D.)

13

Introduction

India after Harsha Vardhan saw the emergence of three important political powers in India from 750 A.D. to 1000 A.D. These were Gurjara Pratiharas in north India, Palas in eastern India and Rashtrakutas in south India (about which we will discuss in next chapter). These powers were constantly fighting with each other with the aim of setting control over Gangetic region in northern India. This armed conflict among these three powers is known as 'Tripartite Struggle'.

The Palas

Sasanka, the contemporary of Harsha Vardhana, had established a powerful empire in Bengal. After his death there prevailed anarchy in Bengal. Hence, the nobles elected Gopala as their leader, who laid the foundation of Pala dynasty in the 8th century. He was a Kshatriya by caste and had proved himself as a successful leader prior to his election as king. He was a devotee of Buddha but he pursued the policy of war and conquest to extend his empire. Under Pala rule Bengal was to enjoy a period of prosperity undreamt of in her early chronicle. Gopala was succeeded by Dharmapala (780-810 A.D.), who greatly expanded the kingdom and was one of the greatest kings that ever ruled in Bengal. When he ascended the throne the Pratiharas and the Rashtrakutas were gradually extending their power towards the east in the desire to possess the plains of north India. Each of them tried to capture Kannauj which was regarded as the main centre of north India at that time. Dharmapala raised Bengal to leading position in North India. He did a lot to restore the greatness of the old imperial city of

Patliputra. Dharmapala was a Buddhist who is also credited for forming the famous Vikramshila University in Bihar. Like Nalanda University, it attracted students from all parts of India and also from Tibet.

Dharmapala was succeeded by his son Devapala (810-50 A.D.). He was a worthy son of a worthy father. He not only maintained his father's empire but also extended it further. Devapala carried out raids in the north, the Deccan, and the peninsula; but thereafter the dynasty declined in power, and Mahendrapala, the Gurjara-Pratihara emperor of Kannauj in the late 9th and early 10th centuries, penetrated as far as northern Bengal. The successors of Devapala proved weak. He was succeeded by Vigrahapala I and then came Narayanapala (854 A.D.-908 A.D.). He was a religious and peaceful man. However, Pala strength was restored by Mahipala I (988 A.D.-1038 A.D.), whose influence reached as far as Varanasi, but on his death the kingdom again weakened. Ramapala (1077 A.D.-1120 A.D.), the last important Pala king, did much to strengthen the dynasty in Bengal and expanded its power in Assam and Orissa; he is the hero of a Sanskrit historical poem, the Ramacarita of Sandhyakara. On his death, however, the dynasty was virtually eclipsed by the rising power of the Senas, though Pala kings continued to rule in southern Bihar for 40 years. The main capital of the Palas appears to have been Mudgagiri (now Munger) in eastern Bihar. The last ruler of Pala dynasty was perhaps Kumarapala. The Palas were supporters of Buddhism, and it was through missionaries from their kingdom that Buddhism was finally established in Tibet.

The Palas ruled over Bihar and Bengal for over four centuries before they disappeared from the stage of history. The most powerful members of the dynasty were no doubt Dharmapala and Devapala. The Pala kingdom suffered decay owing to internal dissensions, revolts and the rise of new power. The Palas were great patrons of art and literature. They took interest in works of public utility.

Vikramshila University

The ancient Indians were much devoted to learning and education. They had established many advanced centres of learning and Vikramshila was one of them. This great seat of learning was founded in the eighth century A.D. by the Pala ruler Dharmapala (780 A.D.-810 A.D.). It was situated near Bhagalpur in Bihar. It remained a famous seat of learning for about four hundred years (8th century to 12th century) of the eastern India. After Nalanda it was the second most important seat of learning in India. Students coming from Tibet and Nepal had a separate arrangement of lodging. The students graduating from this university were held in high respects everywhere. There were six monasteries or colleges and each college there were 108 teachers to impart knowledge in almost all the branches of sciences. The university was well fortified by thick wall like a fort. It had six gates. The Ganga flowed majestically near it. This university of eastern India produced many renowned scholars. It was also a Buddhist seat of learning like Nalanda. Many Sanskrit texts were translated into Tibetan at this monastery. No fees were charged from the students, instead they were provided with free boarding and lodging. The admission was by a test of their courses. There was a wide range of subjects and the students could select subjects according to their choice. Vikramshila was better organised than most other universities. The most celebrated name associated with this university was that of Atisha Dipankara who was greatly respected in Tibet. The university was destroyed in 1203 A.D. by Muhammad Bin Bakhtiyar Khilji who thought it was perhaps some fort. The university was responsible for spreading Indian culture in Tibet and Nepal, etc.

The Pratiharas

The Palas were one of the most long-lived dynasties of Indian history, but their supremacy in the Gangetic Doab was of short duration. It was over thrown by the Pratiharas. The Gurjara Pratihara, was an imperial Indian dynasty that ruled much of Northern India from the 7th to the 11th centuries. At its peak of prosperity and power (*c.* 836 A.D.-910 A.D.), the Gurajara-Pratihara Empire approached or even exceeded the Gupta Empire in the extent of its territory.

The Gurjara Pratihara dynasty was founded by Nagabhatta I in 816 A.D., he ruled first at Ujjain and later at Kannauj. The origin of the Gurjaras is uncertain. However, most historians believe the Gurjaras had an indigenous origin. The name Gurjara does not appear before the end of the 6th century. According to Dr. H.C. Raychaudhuri, "Before the end of the ninth century the power of this new imperial line had extended in all directions and the command of the great Pratihara king was obeyed all over the wide expense of territory stretching from Pehoa in the Punjab to Deogarh in central India, and from Una in Kathiawar to Paharpur in North Bengal."[1]

The Pratiharas involved themselves in a three-cornered contest with the Palas of Bengal and the Rashtrakutas of Deccan. Vatsaraja, Nagabhatta's nephew suffered a great defeat at the hands of the Rashtrakutas, and both he and his son Nagabhata II seem to have accepted Rashtrakuta suzerainty for a time. Nagabhatta I played an important role in the complicated wars of the early 9th century involving Pratiharas, Rashtrakutas, and Palas. With the power of the Rashtrakutas weakened, Nagabhatt I became the most powerful ruler of northern India and established his new capital at Kannauj. Nagabhata I was succeeded by his son Ramabhadra (Ramadeva), who after a brief reign was succeeded by his son Mihira Bhoja about 836 A.D. Nothing particular is recorded about Nagabhatta's successor, Ramabhadra. Under Bhoja and his successor Mahendrapala (Mahendrayudha, reigned *c.* 890 A.D.-910 A.D.), the Pratihara empire reached its peak of prosperity and power. Dr. H.C. Raychaudhuri mentions, "Mahendrapala I imitated Harsha and Yasovarman in encouraging learning".[2] His court was adorned by the poet Rajasekhara.

After the death of Mahendrapala says V.A. Smith, the throne was occupied for two or three years by Bhoja II, elder son of Mahendrapala, who died early, and was succeeded by his half-brother, Mahipala (*c.* 910 A.D.-40 A.D.). The beginning of the decline and fall of the empire of Kannauj dates from his reign. The power of the Pratiharas was apparently weakened by dynastic discord. It was further diminished as a result of a great raid from the Deccan, led by the Rashtrakuta king Indra III, who in about 916 A.D. sacked Kannauj. Under a succession of rather obscure kings, the Pratiharas never regained their former influence. Their feudatories became more and more powerful, one by one throwing off their allegiance until by the end of the 10th century the Pratiharas controlled little more than the Gangetic doab. Their last important king, Rajyapala, was driven from Kannauj by Mahmud of Ghazni in 1018 A.D. and was later killed by the forces of the Chandela king Vidyadhara. For about a generation longer a small Pratihara principality apparently survived in the area of Allahabad. The Pratiharas were the most important dynasty of medieval northern India, and their disappearance marked a stage in the political decline that accompanied the Muslim conquest.

The Rajputs

The breakup of these powers brought about the emergence of many smaller kingdoms all over the country. In the northern India emerged the various Rajput states such as Chahmanas (Chauhans), Chandellas, Parmarasa, etc. The series of invasion by the Huns and other foreign tribes on the fifth and sixth centuries shook the fabric of Hindu society and brought about a re-arrangement of the caste system and of the ruling dynasties. The latter half of the seventh century during which this new grouping of states took place may be regarded as a period of transition from early to medieval India. The most prominent feature of this transitional period is the rise of the Rajput clans. Henceforth, the Rajputs began to play a prominent part in the history of northern and western India. Almost all the kingdoms were ruled by families of Rajputs, hence the period from the death of Harsha to the Muslim Conquest of India may be called the Rajput period (647 A.D. to 1192 A.D.). During this period the unity of the country was completely lost and innumerable petty states which were continually being formed, dissolved and formed again. Most of these states were under the rule of the people called Rajputs. But their origin is contradictory. In this connection different historians hold quite divergent views and bring forward their different theories. Some of the most important theories are discussed below:

(i) **Foreign Origin Theory:** The word Rajput does not occur in early Sanskrit literature nor do we hear of the Rajput clans before the eighth century A.D. This clearly proves that they were a later addition to the population of India. During the troubled times of that followed the breakup of the Gupta Empire many foreign races such as the Huns, the Gurjars, etc. settled in the Punjab and Rajputana and became Indianised in course of time. The upper ranks of these foreigners whose main occupation was war, came to be known as Rajputs while the humbles folk ranked low in social status and developed into inferior castes such as Gurjars, Jats and others. The division of the same class of people was based not on birth but on occupation. The Hinduised descendants of the original invaders who belonged to the ruling classes with war and government as their chief business came to be treated as Kshatriyas. The common people on the other hand took rank or castes of lower degree. Thus, many of the most distinguished Rajput clans such as the Chauhans, the Pratiharas, the Pawars or Parmars, the Solankis or Chalukyas are descended mainly from foreigners called Scythians. The chief advocate of this theory is Colonel Todd, the renowned author of *Rajasthan*. In this book, he has tried to show that with the passage of time these invading tribes such as Kushans, Sakas, Huns and Gurjaras began to marry the Indian women and were got merged in Hinduism. Their leaders or chiefs who had become known because of their strength and courage, organised their separate groups and began to call themselves Rajputs. While those among them who were not powerful and were ordinary people came to be called Jats, Gurjars and Ahirs. This theory of foreign origin has found many supporters including such eminent historians as Crooks and Bhandarkar. One of their agreements in favour of this theory is the practice of worshipping fire which has been taken from the practice of fire worship of the Huns and Sakas. The practices of sacrifice and *asvamedha yajna* and having a special taste for fighting, etc. are also suggested to have come from these foreign war-like tribes especially the Huns. In many other aspects the Rajputs resemble more or less these foreign tribes.

(ii) The Theory of Descent from Kshatriya Heroes: The above theory of foreign origin of the Rajputs is not acceptable to many Indian authors and scholars like Ved Vyas, Vaidya and Gauri Shankar Ojha. They hold that the Rajputs are pure

Aryans and are descendants of the *Sauryavansis* and *Chandravansis* dynasties of the Kshatriyas. In favour of their theory they put forward the following arguments—(a) Most of the customs of the Rajputs very much resemble the customs of Aryans; (b) Their physical structure also resembles the ancient Aryans; (c) The present Rajput rulers of the chief Rajput states like Mewar, Jaipur and Bikaner are still proved of their descent from the ancient Aryans. They regard themselves to be the descendants of the Suryavansi clan founded by Sri Ramchandraji. As for the practice of fire worship, it has been taken from the Aryans and not from the foreigners. The practice of sacrifice, *asvamedha yajna* and love for fighting were inherited by the Rajputs from their Aryan predecessors and not from any foreign tribes. The family traditions and legends all go to prove that the Rajputs are Kshatriya descendants of the Suryavansi (founded by Ram) and Chandravansis dynasties (founded by Lord Krishna).

(iii) **Theory of Descent from the Original Inhabitants of India:** Some scholars are of the view that Rajputs especially living along the Vindhya Hills are descendants of the original inhabitants of India. The Chandella Rajputs of Bundelkhand belong to the Gonds. The renowned Rani Durgavati also belonged to these Gonds. But this theory has not found acceptance of the historians.

(iv) **Agnikul Theory:** Some Rajputs claim their decent from the Agnikula. They say that their ancestors were born of the sacred fire that kindled at Mount Abu. This theory was brought forward by the court poet Chand Bardoi in his work *Prithvi Raj Raso*. It is said that when Parshurama destroyed all the Kshatriyas and there was no one left to protect the Brahmans, the Brahmans themselves kindled the sacred fire at Mount Abu and performed a Yajna lasting for forty days. They prayed to God to produce a warrior class to protect them. Their prayer was granted and out of the *Agnikunda* or fire pit four great heroes sprang up. These four heroes founded the four great families of the Chauhans, Chalukyas, Parmars and the Pratiharas. But some historians do not agree with this theory. They regard all this story just a myth and feel that some sort of sacrifice must have been performed before these warring tribes of the foreigners were taken in the Hindu fold. The legend also shows that the four clans mentioned are all related to one another and that they all arose in Southern Rajputana. Now it has been proved that the Pratiharas are undoubtedly of foreign origin. It is possible that their allied tribes are also similarly descended from foreign sources. The fact seems to be that when a foreign class or tribe became Hinduised its ruling families were recognised as Kshatriyas while the rank and file lost their tribal character and developed into an Indian caste of inferior rank. As all foreigners who came to India became part and parcel of Hinduism so they were given status according to their status.

None of the above theories have found favour with the historians though all of these theories contain some elements of truth in them. Dr. V.A. Smith has come to the conclusion that the Rajputs were the descendants of the foreign invading tribes like the Kushans, Sakas and Huns while the others belonged to the ancient Kshatriya classes.

RAJPUT KINGDOMS

After Harsha's death in 647 A.D. confusion once again reigned supreme and a large number of small states sprang up on the ruins of his empire. The national unity of the country was completely lost. New states were being formed, dissolved and formed again. Most of these new states were under the rules of the Rajputs. At the time of Muslim invasions the whole of northern India was divided into a large number of Rajput Kingdoms, the chief among them were the following:

(i) **The Chauhans in Delhi and Ajmer**: The Chauhans, the most undaunted of the Rajput races, ruled Ajmer. They faced the onslaught of the Muslims under Muhammad of Ghori. Delhi and Ajmer were the most powerful kingdoms of northern India at that time. Ajmer was ruled by the Chauhan chief of the Rajput clans. One of the kings of this dynasty, Vigraharaja, was famous as a poet and patron of Sanskrit literature. His nephew was the famous Prithviraj Chauhan who carried off Jaichand's daughter. He was a warrior prince. He defeated the Chandel

King Parmadi or Parmal as well as Shahabuddin Ghori. The latter however defeated and killed him at the second battle of Tarain (1192 A.D.). Prithviraj is the most popular hero of Northern India and has been immortalised in the songs of bards and epics. The most famous of these is the *Chand Raso* composed by his court poet Chand Bardoi. Delhi was founded in 933 A.D.-934 A.D. In the eleventh century, it was held by the Rajput chiefs of the Tomara clan. Towards the middle of this century one of the Tomara chiefs removed to Delhi the famous iron pillar set up somewhere near Mathura in the fourth century. In the 12th century the city was included in the dominions of Prithviraj Chauhan. Prithviraj Chauhan was a very powerful and brave ruler. It is because of his chivalry and great merit that Sanyukta the daughter of his rival Jaichand of Kannauj began to love him. In 1192 A.D. when Muhammad Ghori invaded India Prithviraj gave him a crushing defeat at the battle of Tarain and forced him to take to his heels. But next year the Rajput army was completely routed and Prithviraj was captured and murdered in cold blood. For a short period Chauhan dynasty continued to rule as petty rulers but was finally subdued soon.

(ii) **The Gaharwars of Kannauj**: The Pratihara dynasty of Kannauj was replaced by the Gaharwar clan of Rajputs. The new dynasty was founded by Chandradeva towards the close of the eleventh century. His grandson Govinda Chandra ruled from 1100 A.D. to 1160 A.D. was an able monarch who tried to restore the past glory of Kannauj. Jaichandra the grandson of Govind Chandra tried to stem the tide of Muslim invasion but was defeated and killed by Mohammad Ghori in 1191 A.D. After this disaster Kannauj ceased to exist as an independent state. Kannauj under Mihir Bhoja (840 A.D.-890 A.D.) was once the premier cities of Northern India. The Pratiharas were defeated by two Rathor Rajputs. Jaichand the last ruler of Kannauj had enmity with Prithviraj Chauhan of Delhi and Ajmer. He encouraged Mohammad Ghori to invade India. Had Jaichand come forward to help Prithvi Raj, Mohammad Ghori could not have succeeded in defeating Prithvi Raj in the battle of Tarain (1192 A.D.). Jaichand was also not spared. Two years later in 1194 A.D. Mohammad Ghori attacked Kannauj and Jaichand was killed in the battle. Thus, Jaichand was paid for his treachery. "With the death of Prithviraj and Jaichand the sun of Hindu glory set for ever" (Prof. N.N. Ghosh) but successors of Jaichand continued to rule and were finally defeated by Iltutmish.

(iii) The Parmars of Malwa: The Parmaras were also important Rajput rulers of this period. They ruled at Malwa. Dhara Munja (974-95 A.D.) had been the most powerful ruler of the Parmar dynasty. He himself was a great scholar and a poet of high order. He was also great patron of art and learning. Another famous ruler of the dynasty was Raja Bhoja (1018-60 A.D.). His military conquests as well as cultural contributions remain notable in the history of Rajputs. He is still famous and his name is associated with many legends. He was a great scholar and author of many books on poetry, architecture and astronomy. He is said to have constructed a beautiful lake near Bhopal and founded a famous Sanskrit college in Dhara. He is a great figure both in history and fables. With his death the greatness of the Parmars was also gone for ever. Bhoja was a great patron of learning and art. There were many scholars of repute in his court. He had formed one city named Bhojpur. He was the worshipper of Lord Shiva. Probably, he had built more than 104 temples. He was a conquerer also which has been testified by an inscription. Under his reign, Malwa was quite prosperous. His successors proved to be weak and incapable of protecting the kingdom.

(iv) The Chandela Dynasty of Bundelkhand: The Chandela dynasty of the Rajputs ruled over Bundelkhand which was situated between the Jamuna and the Narbada. Its capital was Mahoba while Kalinjar was its important fort. Chandelas were probably descendants of Hinduised Gonds. The early Chandel Rajas appeared to have acquired a small principality near Chhatarpur in the central India. In the ninth century they overthrew the neighbouring Pratiharas and pushed the boundaries of their kingdom as far north as the Jamuna. The Chandelas appeared to have been subordinate to the Pratihara King Bhoja of Kannauj but they asserted their independence early in the tenth century. A Chandela King Yashverman defeated Devpala of Kannauj and forced him to give up an image of Vishnu which he enshrined in the temple built by him at Khajuraho. His son Dhanga was the most distinguished king of the dynasty. His reign lasted from 950-90 A.D. His son Gonda took part in the opposition to Sultan Mahmud in the second half of the 11th century. Kirtiverman was another powerful ruler of this dynasty. He repulsed the attack of the Chedi King. He extended the frontiers of his dominions and restored the glory of his House. He was a great patron of art and literature. He is also famous for the Kiret Sagar Lake which he caused to be excavated. The last independent Chandel ruler was Parmal who was defeated by Prithviraj in 1182 A.D. and from whom Kutubuddin captured Kalinjar in 1203 A.D. After the Chandelas sank into obscurity although some of their chiefs continued to rule as local Rajas in some parts of Bundelkhand. Rani Durgawati who fought with Akbar's forces belonged to Chandel dynasty.

The Chandel princes were great builders of temples and forts and constructors of lakes. The magnificent temples at Khajuraho are the best examples of Chandel architecture. These temples now attract tourists from whole world.

(v) **The Sisodia Dynasty of Mewar**: Mewar was under the domination of Sisodia dynasty which continued to rule over this territory up to 1647 A.D. Its capital was Chittor. The founder of this dynasty was Bapa Rawal. However, under Rana Kumbha and his grandson Rana Sanga, Mewar made a great progress. The former defeated the Muslim rulers of Malwa and to commemorate his conquest he built a splendid tower known as "Vijai Stambha" at Chittor. He was also a great scholar, musician and great builder. He is said to have built a large number of forts in Mewar. His grandson Rana Sanga and Maharana Pratap (Rana Sanga's grandson) gave a tough fight to the Mughals. Later on Mewar kings opposed Aurangzeb.

(vi) **The Kaluchuri Dynasty of Chedi**: The state of Chedi was situated between the Narbada and Godavari rivers and was ruled by the Kaluchuri dynasty. The capital of this state was Tripuri near modern Jabbalpure. Like the Chandelas the

Kaluchuris were formerly subordinate to the Pratiharas but about the middle of the 10th century A.D. they asserted their independence. Laxmi Karan was an important ruler of this dynasty who extended his empire all around. But towards the beginning of 12th century A.D. the Chedi possessions were lost to the rising dynasties of the Ganpatis of Warrangal, Yadavas of Devgiri and the Baghela Rajputs.

(vii) **The Senas of Bengal:** The Senas who gave the death blow to the Pala power in Bengal were of Southern origin. The founder of the dynasty was Samanta Sena. The important rulers of this dynasty were Vijaya Sena, Vallala Sena and Lakshman Sena. Lakshman Sena was the last important member of the dynasty. He overran regions of Kamrup and Kalinga. He ruled from 1179 A.D. to 1205 A.D. During the early years of his reign he proved himself to be a great warrior. The inclusion of the Gaya district in his dominions shows that he ousted the Gahadavalas from Magadha. In his old age the kingdom began to fall to pieces owing to the ambitions of local chiefs who set up independent principalities in South and East Bengal. During this period of turnoil Bengal was invaded by Mohammad Bakhtiyar Khilji who made a surprise attack upon Nadia where Lakshman Sena was living at that time. Lakshman Sena fled to Eastern Bengal and continued to rule there three or four years more till 1205 A.D. His son maintained the struggle against the Muslim invaders and preserved their independence in East Bengal till the later half of the 13th century. Lakshmana was a devout Vaishnava. He was a patron of learning and eminent poets like Jayadeva the author of *Gita Govinda* and *Dhoyi* and author of the *Pavanduta* graced his court. Towards the end of the 12th century A.D. (1199 A.D.), one of the generals of Mohammed Ghori, Mohammad Bin Bakhtiyar Khilji invaded Bengal and Bihar and annexed them to the Muslim empire.

Causes of Decline of the Rajputs

It is surprising that the Rajputs failed in establishing a permanent empire in India. They possessed all the necessary resources and courage, but in spite of their outstanding courage they failed miserably in establishing a permanent empire. Constant fighting weakened the Rajputs. They were not conversant with the latest warfare techniques and their mode of fighting and weapons were outdated. Also, they never united against a common enemy. The feudal system also proved disastrous for the Rajputs. Their lack of political foresight and constant rivalries prevented any combined opposition to the Muslim invaders.

Political Condition

The state structure in this period has often been described as "decentralized" political system. It is a system in which there is of course a king as the main authority at the top, but he shares his rule with other small chiefs called feudatories. There was complete lack of political unity. The whole country was divided into small independent states that were undermining their strength in mutual jealousies and quarrels. There was lack of farsightedness and political insight. The evils of caste system were coming to the surface. Kshatriyas was the only class of soldiers to defend the frontiers. They could never give a joint and united fight in repulsing the invaders. The political organization of the Rajputs was based on the feudal system. The land was distributed among his various landlords who paid him the fixed annual revenues and also rendered his military service at the time of need. This system was most defective as it would often lead to revolts and conspiracies. The Rajputs were undoubtedly brave, courageous, patriotic and chivalrous, but they lacked political insight. For example they would not attack the running enemy nor would they fight an unarmed man. Mohammad Ghori was defeated by Prithvi Raj Chauhan of Delhi but he was allowed to go free which proved disastrous. Such high ideals seldom pay in warfare. The Rajput army was not well organised and trained. It comprised of infantry, cavalry and elephants. The elephants instead of any help often proved a great source of weakness. When they were out of control they trampled their own men and caused destruction. The organisation of the army was quite unscientific. The rulers had very small personal army. Feudal lords supplied soldiers at the time of emergency. The soldiers were not properly trained and equipped. They were also not loyal to the king. Administration of justice of the Rajput rulers was praiseworthy. The king himself was the supreme judge. He considered it his duty to give justice to the people. Justice was unexpensive and quick. The main source of income to the royal treasury was the annual tax payable from the feudal lords. Besides presents, gifts, fines, income from various taxes on trade and industry were other sources of state income. The taxes on the people were light, so it was not sufficient for defence against foreign invaders. For proper administration the kingdom was divided into provinces. Each *Bhukti* or province was under the charge of an *uprik*. A *Bhukti* was further divided into districts under an officer called *Vishayapati*. The officials were not paid in cash but given land grants according to the position of the officer concerned.

Social Condition

The society was divided into many castes and sub-castes. Instead of traditional four castes now many new castes and sub-castes has emerged in the society. The castes had great influence on social customs, ceremonies, worship, marriages and eating habits, etc. Large number of foreigners had also settled in the country. They were all absorbed in different castes. Many new castes were born on the basis of professions. A new caste of *Kayasthas* originated. The people of this caste were mainly government servants and their main work was writing. The caste system had grown very rigid and narrow. The different castes had their different rules and customs. The Rajputs were very proud of their high descent from the Aryan heroes like Rama (Suryavanshi) and Krishna (Chandravanshi). No doubt they were very brave and chivalrous and would never show their backs in the battlefield. Even if the most bitter enemy sought their protection, they would treat him most generously. The women were held in high respect. They honoured their women and staked their lives to protect them and their honour. But a change was noticeable. They were gradually losing their traditional high position. They had to observe strict *purdah*. Rajput women were not behind their men-folk in bravery and courage. Rani Laxmi Bai, Rani Durgawati, Tarabai, Ahliya Bai and Padmini, etc. proved great warriors and diplomats and rulers. They were devotedly loyal to their husbands and performed the *sati* sacrifice willingly.

Character of the People: Generally, the people were very honest and hard working, trustworthy and hospitable. The Rajputs were held in high respect as the defenders of the country. Mostly, the people were farmers, artisans and businessmen. They lived in villages a simple life. They were generally contented and happy. They were god fearing and worshipped a large number of gods and goddesses. The upper classes of people especially the Rajputs ruling class and their feudal lords led a very luxurious life. They were very fond of wine and opium and were inclined towards pleasure, but common people lead a simple and moral life.

Marriages: The inter-caste marriages were seldom. Early marriage was the general custom. The marriage was arranged by the parents and elderly people among the people of their own caste. The caste system was getting more and more rigid. Widow marriage was not regarded well. The widows led a miserable life. The feudal lords and courtiers generally had more than one wife. The birth of a girl in the house was not regarded auspicious. The newly born girls were killed among the Rajputs, but common people cared for both boys and girls.

Religious Condition

The Rajputs were strict followers of Hinduism. There were mainly three religions prevalent in the society—Hinduism, Buddhism and Jainism. The Rajputs were follower of Hinduism. Buddhism was on the decline and the Hinduism made a great progress under the Rajput rulers. They worshipped Lord Shiva, Vishnu and Goddess Durga. They built large number of beautiful temples. They were great patron of art and architecture. There were many Hindu festivals which were celebrated with great pomp and show. Some of these festivals were Holi, Diwali and Dussehra, etc. Hindus regarded it their duty to visit holy places and make pilgrimages to Badrinath, Kedarnath, Kashi, Hardwar, Allahabad, Puri, Amarnath, Dwarka, etc. and other holy places of pilgrimage. The study of holy books like *Ramayana*, *Mahabharata* and *Gita* became very popular under the Rajputs. The women observed many fasts and prayed for the long lives and prosperity of their husbands. The Rajputs were very fond of warfare and, therefore, they could not reconcile themselves to the doctrine of Ahimsa of the Buddhists and Jains. The result was that both these religions suffered a great setback in the Rajput period. It was also during this period that great religious scholars and preachers like Kumarul Bhatta and Shankracharya made their best attempt to revive Hinduism. They made vehement attacks on Jainism and Buddhism and by their whirl in tours and discourses gave a death blow to the two faiths. Consequently, both Buddhism and Jainism began to decline rapidly and Hinduism revived during the Rajput period. It was a great period of renaissance of Hinduism. Most of the population embraced Hinduism.

Art and Literature

During the Rajput period the Indian masons and craftsmen produced beautiful works of art. The Rajput rulers were great patrons of art and literature. They were great builders of beautiful palaces, forts, temples and other works of art. Their irrigation works, tanks and lakes, bathing ghats, reservoirs and fortresses testify to their skill of engineering and architecture— "Fortress of Chittor, Ranthambhore, Mandu and Gwalior, Kalinjar, etc. are conspicuous examples of their architectural skill". The castle of Jodhpur which stands on a lofty and inaccessible rock and overlooks the town still excites our curiosity for its architectural design and wonderful execution. The Rajput rulers laid the foundation of many beautiful cities and built a large number of palaces by the side of beautiful lakes surrounded by natural scenes. There are a large number of temples which were built by the Rajput rulers. They amply testify to the artistic table of architecture and sculpture. The Linga Raja temple of Bhuvneshwar (Orissa) is a fine example of the medieval Hindu temples of Northern India. It has a spire of 180 feet high rising imposingly above the surrounding buildings. Another example is Mahadeva Temple of Khajuraho. It is renowned for its lofty spire, beautiful sculpture and other decorations. Tejpal temple at Mount Abu is a class of its own. It is a fine example of Rajput art. There are a large number of Jain temples also which gives the expression of the medieval Hindu architecture. The Tejpal temple built of pure white marble and show excellent and delicate workmanship. Its central dome has won admiration of people from all over the world. There are lot of temples built all over India.

Literature: The Rajput kings were great patrons of learning. Learned scholars adorned their courts. There was allround development of Sanskrit. Most of the books were written in Sanskrit language. The writers of outstanding works were encouraged by the Rajput rulers. Side by side of development of Sanskrit, regional languages also developed and many books of highment were written in different languages. Hindi, Gujarati, Bangla, etc. developed greatly and produced works of high merits.

Literary Men and Their Works: Bhavabhuti, Kalhan, Jayadeva, Jagnaik Ghagh, Raj Shekhar, etc. are names which shine brilliantly on the horizon of literature. Bhavabhuti was a dramatist of the highest order. He produced *Malti Madhava*, *Mahavir Charita*, and *Uttar Ramcharit* which can easily be ranked with Kalidas dramas. Kalhan's *Rajtarangini* is a historical work. Jayadeva's *Gita Govinda* is the immortal work of this period. Raj Shekhar's *Karpur Manjari* and *Kavya Mimmansa* are other important works of the Rajput period. Jagnaik wrote *Allahakhand*, Chand Bardoi's *Prithvi Raj Raso* during this period. *Kathasaritasagara* by Somadeva was another important Sanskrit work.

Education: The education system was based on the 'Gurukul system'. The students were imparted education in the Guru's Ashram which were generally far away from the crowded towns in the lap of nature. Temples and monasteries were also great seats of learning. Nalanda was the most renowned centre of learning. The students flocked here from far and wide to get higher education under the guidance of renowned 'Acharyas'. The other centres of learning were Odantpuri (Bihar), Sompuri (Bengal) and Vikramshilla (East Bihar).

Painting and Music: The Rajput kings were very fond of music, dance and painting. All the fine arts found excellent changes of development. Musicians and dancers got patronage, encouragement and help at the hands of the Rajput rulers. Many great philosophers and religious reformers like Kumarul

Bhatta and Shankracharya flourished and preached during this period. This was the time when Rajput monarchs vied with each other in magnificence and number of temples. Skilled artisans were diverted from other pursuits to the pious labour of elaborating the embellishment of the temple service in stone.

IMPORTANT QUESTIONS

1. Discuss the Tripartite struggle among the Pratiharas, the Palas and the Rashtrakutas for the sovereignty of Kannauj.
2. Who were the Rajputs? Discuss different opinions concerning their origin.
3. Discuss in brief the different Rajput kingdoms emerged in the north India in the 7th century A.D.

NOTES

1. Dr. H.C. Raychaudhuri, *An Advanced History of India*, p. 160.
2. *Ibid.*, p. 161.

REFERENCES

Chaurasia, R.S., *History of Ancient India* (*Earliest times to 1200 A.D.*), New Delhi: Atlantic Publishers, 2008.

E notes, National Institute of Open Learning.

Encyclopedia Britannica.

Raychaudhuri, H.C., *An Advanced History of India*, New Delhi: Macmillan Publishers, 1978.

Sharma. L.P., *History of Ancient India* (*Pre-historic Age to 1200 A.D.*), New Delhi: Konark Publishers, 1999.

Smith, V.A., *The Early History of India*, New Delhi: Atlantic Publishers, 1999.

History of Deccan and South India

14

Introduction

The Neolithic period of south India was succeeded by the megalithic cultures (1200 B.C.-300 B.C.), about which we have already discussed in the third chapter. The megalithic culture in south India is followed by the Sangam age. The Sangam age refers to that period in the early history of south India when large numbers of poems in Tamil were composed by a number of authors. Our knowledge of the earliest south Indian history from 300 B.C.-300 A.D. can be traced from the Sangam literature. It was produced by poets who joined together in assemblies (Sangam) patronized by chiefs and kings during the first four centuries of the Christian era. The Sangam literature was secular in nature. Only a part of the Sangam literature has been discovered so far which has been compiled into several texts. It also gives portrayal of the contemporary society and culture of Tamilaham or Tamil region and its peaceful interaction with the northern culture and the foreign countries. This region stretches between the hills of Tirupati and the tip of Kanyakumari. The dynasties under which this literature flourished are the Cholas with their capital at Uraiyur, the Cheras with their capital at Vanji, and the Pandyas with their capital at Madurai. Though some scholars regard the Sangam literature as imaginative, yet the descriptions mentioned in the literature are confirmed by the archaeological excavations and accounts of foreign travellers.

We have references to the Cholas, Cheras, and Pandyas in the inscriptions of Asoka and Kharavela, and in the *Indica* of Magasthenese. In the 4th century B.C., the Greek ambassador at the court of Chandragupta Maurya had mentioned about the Pandya state. It has been given in the *Hathi-gumpha* inscription of king Kharvela of Kalinga that he defeated the confederacy of three rulers of extreme south India. Thus, it is clear that these three states of south India existed among ancient states of India. There were frequent conflicts between the Cheras, Cholas and the Pandyas, which gave large scope to the Sangam poets to compose poems on war.

The Cheras

The Cheras ruled over parts of modern Kerala. Their capital was Vanji and their important seaports were Tondi and Musiri. Together with the Cholas and the Pandyas, they formed the three principle warring Iron Age Tamil kingdoms in India. Cheras ruled from before the Sangam Age (3rd century B.C. to 3rd century A.D.) until the 12th century A.D. Their kingdom extended over the Malabar Coast, Karur, Coimbatore and Salem districts in south India, which now is a part of present-day Kerala and Tamil Nadu. Very little is known about the early history of the Cheras. Vanji, identified with the present-day Karur in Tamil Nadu, was the capital of the Cheras and also an important centre of trade and craft. They had flourishing trade relations with the Romans. It is confirmed by the recovery of a large number of Roman gold coins in south India. Roman ships loaded with gold used to come here to take back large amounts of pepper. The first known ruler among the Chera rulers was Udiyanajerala. He was succeeded by his son Nedum Cheralatan who transformed the Chera dynasty into a powerful one and extended and enriched his kingdom from all aspects. The Chera rulers referred in the Sangam literature, Elanjerala and Manderanjerala fought against the contemporary Chola and Pandya rulers respectively. The last known Chera ruler, Cheraman Perumal converted to Islam and built the first mosque in India.

The Cholas

The Chola kingdom of the Sangam period extended from modern Tiruchi district to southern Andhra Pradesh. Their capital was first located at Uraiyur and then shifted to Puhar.

The history of Cholas falls into four periods, the early Cholas, the interregnum period, medieval Cholas and Chalukya Cholas. The Chola Kingdom is very ancient, there has been references made in *Mahabharata* and even in Asokan inscriptions. The earliest Chola kings for whom there is concrete evidence are mentioned in the Sangam literature. Among the early Chola rulers mentioned in the Sangam literature, the most marked is Karikala. He is credited with constructing a dam on the river Kaveri. It is considered to be the earliest dam in the country. He carved out an independent kingdom of his own towards the end of the second century A.D. by defeating the Cheras, the Pandyas and the Ceylonese ruler. Karikala's successors were not so powerful and so the dynasty suffered an eclipse about the 3rd and 4th century. The rise of the Pallavas and the aggressions of the Pandyas and Cheras were mostly responsible for this eclipse of the Cholas. There is not much information around three centuries from the end of the Sangam Age. An obscure dynasty, the Kalabhras invaded Tamil country and ruled for around three centuries. They were displaced by the Pallavas and Pandyas around 6th century.

After a long period of obscurity till the 9th century A.D. the Cholas regained their lost glory under Vijalaya (846 A.D.-871 A.D.), a feudatory of the Pallavas. He established the imperial line of the medieval Cholas. There is an abundance of materials from diverse sources on the medieval Cholas. A large number of stone inscriptions and copper plate grants have been instrumental in constructing the history of medieval Cholas. The Chola dynasty was at its peak of its influence and power during the medieval period. Through their leadership and vision, kings such as Rajaraja I and his son Rajendra I extended the Chola kingdom beyond the traditional limits of Tamil Kingdom. A famous work composed in the regional language around this time under the Cholas was the Tamil version of the *Ramayana*, composed by Kamban.

Rajaraja I (985A.D.-1014 A.D.)

The Chola king Rajaraja I made a successful use of his navy and conquered not only Maldive and Lakshadweep Islands but also Sri Lanka. The invasion of Sri Lanka was entrusted to his son Rajendra I. Another achievement of Rajaraja I was over the growing power of the western Chalukyas of Kalyani. Satyasraya was defeated and Rajaraja I captured the Raichur Doab, Banavasi and other places. Hence, the Chola power extended up to the river Tungabadra. They also overpowered the kings of Malaya and Java and Sumatra. One of the greatest contributions of Rajaraja I was the construction of the famous temple known as Rajarajeshwara or Brihadesvara temple, dedicated to Shiva at Tanjore. The walls of the temple are engraved with the story of his victories till the twenty-sixth year of his reign. Although himself a worshipper of Siva, he was sufficiently liberal-minded to endow a Burmese Buddhist temple at the port of Nagapatam, where two such temples continued to be the object of foreign pilgrimages until the fifteenth century. He also ordered a survey of land for better collection of land revenue in his empire.

Rajendra I (1014 A.D.-44 A.D.)

The rule of his son, Rajendra I was even more impressive. Mahinda V, the king of Sri Lanka attempted to recover from the Cholas the northern part of Ceylon. Rajendra I defeated him and seized the southern Sri Lanka. Thus, the whole of Sri Lanka was made part of the Chola Empire. His most famous military enterprise was his expedition to north India. He carried his arms up to Ganga in Bengal after defeating the Pala King, Mahipala. To solemnize his victory he founded a new capital called 'Gangaikondacholapuram' and acquired for himself the title "Gangai-Konda" (conqueror of Ganga). He reasserted the Chola authority over the Chera and Pandya countries. He was a great patron of learning and was known as Pandita-Chola.

The last important Chola king was Kullotunga (1070 A.D.-1122 A.D.). Under him the Chola Empire started disintegrating and shrunk to much smaller area.

Administration Under Imperial Cholas

The system of Chola administration was highly organised and efficient. The Cholas had three major administrative divisions called Central Government, Provincial Government and Local Government. Tanjore was the capital of the Cholas. The efficient Chola administrative system has been well appreciated by many historians and rulers.

(i) **Central Government:** The king was the head of the administration. The Chola kingship was hereditary. The heir to the throne was called Yuvaraja. The Chola monarchs enjoyed enormous powers and privileges and took up titles which marked their achievements. They undertook royal tours to increase the efficiency of the administration. There was elaborate administrative machinery comprising various officials called perundanam and sirudanam.

(ii) **Provincial Government:** The Chola Empire was divided into nine provinces. They were also called Mandalams. The head of the province was called viceroy. The royal princes or officers were incharge of Mandalams. The Viceroys were in constant touch with the Central Government. The viceroys had a large number of officials to assist them in the work of administration. Generally, Mandalams were named after the original names or the titles of the Chola kings. Each Mandalam was divided into number of Nadus. Each Nadu was further divided into a number of village unions called Kurrams or Kottams. Every Kurrams was further divided into Urs or villages which form part of the last unit of the administration. Uttaramerur inscriptions speak about the administration of the Cholas.

(iii) **Village Assemblies:** The Chola administrative system was based on democratic principles and most of the government business was carried on by the popular assemblies elected by the people. The Kurrams and the villages enjoyed self-government and vast powers. They had a say in management of their local affairs. The village sabha controlled all the revenues and made necessary payments. The assembly was also responsible for the maintenance of law and order.

(iv) **Military Administration:** The Cholas had organized a powerful army comprising foot soldiers, horsemen, elephants and naval fleet. About seventy regiments were mentioned in the inscriptions. The royal troops were called *Kaikkolaperumpadai*. The Chola army had 60,000 elephants. Very costly Arabian horses were imported to strengthen the cavalry. The Chola army and navy together had 1,50,000 trained soldiers. The armies of the tributary chieftains also joined Chola army at the time of need. Generally, the Chola army was led by the King or Yuvaraja. The Cholas paid special attention to their navy. The naval achievements of the Tamils reached its climax under the Cholas. They controlled the Malabar and Coromandal coasts.

(v) Revenue and Expenditure: The chief source of income of the government was the land tax which was generally 1/6th of the gross produce. It was payable either in cash or kind. The other sources of revenue were salt tax, customs, profession tax, water cess, fines, etc. The Chola rulers spent a major portion of the income on the welfare of their subjects.

Art Under the Cholas

The Cholas who displaced the Pallavas in south India were mighty builders. The Chola art is characterized by a massive grandeur. The large structures were decorated with minute sculptures involving immense labour. Another feature of the Chola art was the addition of a huge gateway called a *Gopurams*. The third feature of the Chola art in addition to *Gopurams* is the pillared halls and long colonnades of the temples. Visitors are wonder struck by the sight of the beautiful and massive temples at Rameshwaram, and Srirangam. The Dravidian style was developed and almost perfected under them. The best example of this style is furnished by the great *Shiva* temple at Tanjore built by Rajaraja the great. The great Shikhara consisting of fourteen storeys rises to a height of 100 ft and it crowned by a massive dome consisting of a single block of stone. It is said that this huge block was carried to the immense height by being rolled along an inclined road about four miles long specially built for the purpose. The massive building is covered from the base to the top with sculpture and decorative mouldings. It occupies the centre of a courtyard with other subsidiary chapels. There was another massive temple at Gangai Kondacholapuram, the new capital city built by Rajendra I in the Trichnopoly district. The city was also adorned with a magnificent palace and a vast artificial lake with stone embankment. All these are now in ruins, but depict their greatness. The other specimens of Chola art are the temples of Vijayalaya-Cholesvara, the Nagesvara temple, the Koranganatha temple and the Muvarakovitna temple.

The Cholas also made great improvement in the art of sculpture making. The best contribution in this respect was the bronze images of Nataraja. These images of Siva in his cosmic dance represent unmatched rhythm and balance.

Chola Bronze Nataraja Statue

Source: Wikipedia

The Pandyas

The Pandyas ruled over the present-day southern Tamil Nadu. Their capital was Madurai. The earliest kings of the Pandyan dynasty were Nediyon, Palyagasalai Mudukudumi Peruvaludhi and Mudathirumaran. The state of Pandyas is referred to in Megasthanese account and is also mentioned in Asoka's inscription. From the records of Greek historian Strabo, we come to know that the Pandyas had maintained trade relations with the Roman Empire in the first century B.C. In the middle of the 7th century A.D. when Hiuen Tsang visited the south, the Pandyas were under the suzerainty of the Pallavas of

Kanchi and Buddhism was quite extinct there. Towards the close of the 9th century A.D. the Pandyas joined hands with the Cholas against the Pallavas and after defeating them, they won their freedom. But in the 11th century A.D. the Pandyas had to bow before the might of the Cholas. It was after the fall of the Cholas, that the Pandyas became the leading power in the south.

The Pandyas were perhaps the oldest among the Sangam Tamil ruling dynasties. In legend and early literature we hear of a Pandyan king called Vadimbalambaninra Pandyan. He was also called Nediyon. He was the first Pandya king who started the worship of ocean. It is said that he ruled from Madurai which was lost in the course of erosion by the sea. He was one of the most reputed and remembered among proto-historic kings of the Pandyan dynasty.

The later Pandyas (1150 A.D.-1350 A.D.) entered their golden age under Maravman Sundara and Jatavarman Sundara Pandyan, who expanded the empire into Telugu country, conquered Kalinga (Orrisa) and invaded and conquered Sri Lanka. They also had extensive trade links with Southeast Asian maritime empires of Sri Vijaya and their successors. During their history, the Pandyas were repeatedly in conflict with the Pallavas, Cholas, Hoysalas and finally the Muslim invaders from the Delhi Sultanate. The Pandyas excelled in both trade and literature before the Christian era. They controlled the pearl fisheries among the South Indian coast, between Sri Lanka and India, which produced some of the finest pearls in the known ancient world. With the fall of the Tamil power at the hands of Malik Kafur in 1310 A.D., the Pandya kingdom started declining. But when the Vijaya Nagar Empire became all powerful in the south, it also absorbed the Pandya state within its boundaries in the 16th century A.D. Thus, ended the Pandya state.

Sangam Polity

Hereditary monarchy was the form of government during the Sangam period. The emperor was the pivot on which turned the whole machinery of the state. But the rulers did not become despots. The king had also taken the advice of his minister and court-poet. The imperial court or *avai* was attended by a number of chiefs and officials. The king was assisted by a large body of officials who were divided into five councils. They were ministers (*amaichar*), priests (*anthanar*), military commanders (*senapathi*), envoys (*thuthar*) and spies (*orrar*). The military administration was also efficiently organized during the Sangam Age. Each ruler had a regular army and their respective Kodimaram (tutelary tree). The kingdom was divided into a number of Provinces (*Mandalam*) under the charge of viceroys. They were persons of royal family. The provinces were sub-divided into divisions (*Kottams*) and the other units of administration like districts.

Land revenue was the chief source of state's income while custom duty was also imposed on foreign trade. The *Pattinappalai* refers to the custom officials employed in the seaport of Puhar. Booty captured in wars was also a major income to the royal treasury. Roads and highways were well maintained and guarded night and day to prevent robbery and smuggling. The king was expected to observe a strict moral code of conduct. He was expected to treat his subjects like his children and provide justice. The king was also expected to encourage fine arts, religion and literature. The king was also expected to engage himself in wars for conquest.

Sangam Society

Though the concept of *varna* was known, social classes in the Sangam period were not marked by higher or lower rankings as in north India. The caste system was not fully accepted and social divisions were primarily based on the basis of one's occupation. Yet, the Brahmanas and the Kshatriyas enjoyed better status in the society. War heroes occupied a special position in society, and memorial stones called *nadukal* or *virukkal* were raised in honour of those who died while fighting. The rich lived in well decorated and big houses. They wore expensive clothes, while the poor lived in small mud huts and had scanty clothes to wear. There were no untouchables in the society but the status of the poor people had worsened.

Eight types of marriages were known to Sangam people and marriage was religious institution. The position of women was better than in the north. They appear to have been educated. It is testified by many poems contributed by women poets to the Sangam literature. Women were engaged in various economic activities such as cattle rearing, spinning, etc. Gradually, their position deteriorated and the cruel practice of Sati could be seen. It was known as *tippayadal* in Tamil. However, it was not obligatory as there are references to widow present in society.

Economic Condition

Sangam Age people were engaged in various economic activities such as agriculture, cattle rearing, crafts and trade. The Sangam literature refers that the far south was very prosperous. The fact is further authenticated by other literary sources and archaeological evidences. Paddy formed the main part of people's diet. It also served as medium of exchange in trade. Variety of herbs, wood and other articles were obtained from forests. Craft included spinning and weaving of textiles especially silk. Salt manufacture was another important activity. Trade with Roman Empire was flourishing; it has been confirmed by the recovery of a large number of Roman gold coins in south India. Roman ships loaded with gold used to come here to take back large amount of pepper. Sangam Age people also maintained trade relations with Egypt, Arabia and China as well as with the countries of South-East Asia. The most important ports were Kaveripattinam, Arikaedu and Vasavasamudra.

Culture of Sangam Age

The Sangam Age in India witnessed the rapid development of literary works in the southern regions. The literature that was created during this time came to be known as Sangam literature. The great poets and writers of this age have left behind invaluable accounts of brilliant literature that continue to charm historians and scholars. Poetry, music and dancing were popular among the people of the Sangam Age. Liberal donations were given to poets by the kings, chieftains and nobles. The royal courts were crowded with singing bards called *Panar* and *Viraliyar*. They were experts in folk songs and folk dances. The arts of music and dancing were highly developed. Dancing was performed by *Kanigaiyar*. *Koothu* was the most popular entertainment of the people.

The literature consists of short and long poems in praise of various heroes, written probably to be recited in the courts. It also constitutes the epics called *Silpadikaraṃ* and *Manimekali*. One of the earliest written scriptures in Tamil grammar is known as *Tolkappiyam*. Another work known as *Ettutogai* or Eight Anthologies is considered to be a fantastic product of the Sangam Age. Many poems were composed during this age and some of the famous ones are Akananuru, Purananuru, etc. These poems speak about the political, social, cultural and traditional aspects of life during the Sangam Age. Some poems also mention the fact that the Cheras formed a vital trading centre with Rome. Some of the great poets who deserve a mention are Avvaiyar, Kapilar, Mamulanar, Paramer, Gautamanar, etc.

The Pallavas

The period of big empire was begun in south India by the Satavahanas. They remained in power till the early 3rd century A.D. After the collapse of the Satavahanas, Ikshvakus rose to power in the Krishna-Guntur region. They were superseded by the Pallavas. In northern Maharashtra and Vidharba the Satavahanas were succeeded by the Vakatakas. They in turn, were followed by the Chalukyas of Badami. After two centuries they were overthrown by their feudatories, the Rashtrakutas in 757 A.D.

From about the fourth to the eighth century the Pallava dynasty plays a great part in the history of southern India. The Pallavas established their kingdom in Tondaimandalam with its capital at Kanchipuram. Pallava dynasty ruled the northern part of Tamil Nadu and the southern part of Andhra Pradesh of present-day India. They established themselves as a notable rising power in the region during 350 A.D. and by the beginning of the seventh century, the Pallavas along with the Chalukyas of Badami and the Pandyas of Madurai, emerged to be the three major states of southern India. Pallavas rule continued till Tondaimandalam was captured and annexed by the Imperial Cholas in the beginning of the tenth century A.D.

The origin of the Pallavas is one of the most distressed problems of ancient history. The name Pallava resembles

Pahlava so closely that most writers have been disposed to favour the hypothesis that Pallavas and Pahlavas were identical, and that consequently the southern Pallava dynasty of Kanchi should be considered as ultimately of Persian origin. But recent research has failed to adduce any historical facts in support of that notion. Another theory is that the Pallavas were of indigeneous growth and came to power after the dissolution of the Andhra Empire. Another view was that the Pallavas were a branch of the Brahmin royal dynasty of the Vakatakas of the Deccan. The fourth view relates the Pallavas with the descendants of the Chola prince and a Naga princess whose native was the island of Manipallavam. A writer says that the Pallavas were the feudatory chieftains of the Satavahanas. According to V.A. Smith, "The origin and affinities of the Pallavas remain obscure." In fact, nothing definite can be said about the origin of the Pallavas. But majority scholars agree that they were the feudatories of the Andharas, who declared their independence and came to power in about the middle of the fourth century A.D.

The discovery of copper plate charters in Prakrit from the time of Shivakanda Varman, who ruled probably about the beginning of the 4th century A.D. His dominions extended from the river Krishna and up to the Bellary district. He belonged to the Bharadvaja gotra, performed a number of Brahmanical sacrifices and bore the title *dhamma-maharajadhiraja*. His successor was his son, Buddha Varman, who in turn was succeeded by Buddhyankura born to his queen Charudevi. After him there is a gloomy period broken by the appearance of Vishnugopa of Kanchi, who was one of the twelve kings of *dakshinapatha* annihilated by Samudragupta. Then came Simha Vishnu who extended his sway up to Kaveri at the cost of Cholas. He claims to have inflicted defeats on the kings of Ceylon and the three Tamil states. He was a devotee of Vishnu.

Simha Vishnu was succeeded by his son Mahendra Varman I in about the beginning of 7th century A.D. He contributed to the greatness of the Pallava dynasty. Some of the most glitzy monuments at Mamallapuram, especially those dedicated to the Hindu god Shiva, were constructed under his rule. He was born a Jain although later converted to Shaivism. He was a great patron of art and architecture and is known for introducing a new style to Dravidian architecture, which is referred to as "Mahendra style". Mahendra Varman also wrote plays, including *Mattavilasa-prahasana* (*The Delight of the Drunkards*), a satire in Sanskrit, which defames Buddhism. He also built irrigation works. Mahendra Varman was defeated by Pulakesin II and the territory of Vengi was given over to Pulakesin. Mahendra Varman's successor, Narasimha Varman I ruled upto 668 A.D. He was the most famous Pallava ruler. He conquered some of the territory that was lost during numerous Pallava-Chalukya battles. He defeated Pulakesin II in three battles. He captured Vatapi the capital of Pulakesin II. King Narasimha Varman also defeated the Pandyas, the Cholas and the Cheras. After his death in about 645 A.D. the Pallava Empire began to fall with a rapid speed, but the rule continued. Later, in 740 A.D., Badami Chalukya ruler Vikramaditya II ended the Pallava sovereignty in southern India permanently and the Pallava dominions were passed to the Chola kings in 9th century A.D.

Administration of the Pallavas

The Pallavas had a well organized administrative system like that of the great Guptas. The head of the state was the king who was called *Maharaj* or *Dharamraj*. The polity was a hereditary kingship and he was assisted and advised by a council of ministers. Although all powers were concentrated in the king's hands, yet he was not a despot. His primary duty was to look after the welfare of his subjects and performed his duty according to ancient *Rajya Dharma*. He maintained a well-trained army. He provided land-grants to the temples known as *Devadhana* and also to the Brahmans known as *Brahmadeya*. The empire was divided into Kottams and villages for administrative convenience. It was also the responsibility of the Central Government to provide irrigation facilities to the lands. A number of irrigation tanks were dug by the Pallava kings. The irrigation tanks at Mahendravadi and Mamandoor were dug during the reign of Mahendravarman I. Detailed information on the tax system could also be traced from the Pallava inscriptions. Land tax was the primary source of the government revenue. There were about eighteen kinds of taxes which the people had to pay, but taxes were light and were used for welfare of people. The *Brahmadeya* and *Devadhana* lands were exempted from tax. The Pallava inscriptions throw much light on the village assemblies called *sabhas* and their committees. They maintained records of all village lands, looked after local affairs and managed temples. The Pallavas had succeeded in providing an efficient and good administration to their empire.

Society and Religion Under the Pallavas

The Tamil society witnessed a great change during the Pallava period. The caste system became rigid. The Brahmins occupied a high place in the society. They were given land-grants by the kings and nobles. They were also given the responsibility of looking after the temples. The Pallavas were the devotees of Hinduism. Thus, Buddhism and Jainism declined during this period. However, some Pallava rulers encouraged Jainism also. Mahendra Varman I was the follower of Jainism faith but later on he came under the influence of Acharya Appar and became a devout Saiva. They performed different *yajnas* and constructed temples and images of different Hindu gods and goddesses like Vishnu, Siva, Brahma, Lakshmi, etc. The Saiva Nayanmars and the Vaishnava Alwars contributed to the growth of Saivism and Vaishnavism. This is known as the Bhakti Movement. They composed their hymns in the Tamil language. These hymns revealed the importance of devotion or Bhakti. The construction of temples by the Pallava kings paved the way for the spread of these two religions.

Education and Literature

The Pallavas supported Buddhism, Jainism, and the Brahminical faith and were patrons of music, painting, and literature. Their capital Kanchi was an ancient centre of learning. The *Ghatika* at Kanchi was popular and it attracted students from all parts of India and abroad. Dignaga, a Buddhist philosopher visited Kanchi in search of knowledge. Instead of Tamil they encouraged Sanskrit and made it their court language. All the Pallava inscriptions are in Sanskrit language. The founder of the Kadamba dynasty, Mayurasarman studied Vedas at Kanchi. Dharmapala, who later became the Head of the Nalanda University, belonged to Kanchi. Bharavi, the great Sanskrit scholar lived in the time of Simhavishnu. Dandin, another Sanskrit writer adorned the court of Narasimhavarman II. Mahendravarman I himself was a great scholar and a writer of high merits. He composed the Sanskrit play *Mattavilas Prahasanam.* Probably, Bhas also produced *Natakaveli* at this time. Tamil literature had also developed. During their reign could be seen the growth of Tamil bhakti literature. The Nayanmars and Alwars composed religious hymns in Tamil. The *Devaram* composed by Nayanmars and the *Nalayradivya Prabandam* composed by Alwars represent the religious literature of the Pallava period. Perundevanar was patronized by Nandivarman II and he translated the *Mahabharata* as *Bharathavenba* in Tamil. *Nandikkalambagam* was another important work but the name of the author of this work is not known. Music and dance also developed during this period. Hiuen Tsang who visited Kanchi in 640 A.D. writes: "The learned were held in high esteem. There were 10,000 Buddhist monks and many Jains. Kanchi was a fine well built city in five miles rounds."

Pallava Art and Architecture

The Pallava rulers were great patrons of art and architecture. It was a great age of temple building. The Pallavas introduced the art of excavating temples from the rock. In fact, the Dravidian style (the southern style of architecture) of temple architecture began with the Pallava rule. It was a gradual evolution starting from the cave temples to monolithic *rathas* and culminated in structural temples. These temples are built in four different designs which are as follows:

(a) **Mahendra Style:** The temples are cut out of a single big rock boulder. Cubical pillars, circular *lingams* and the existence of *Devapalas* at the gates. The rock cut temples at Mandagappattu, Mahendravadi, Mamandur, Dalavanur, Tiruchirappalli, Vallam, Siyamangalam and Tirukalukkunram represent this cave style.

(b) **Mahamalla Style:** The second stage is represented by the monolithic *rathas* and *mandapas*. Narasimhavarman I took the credit for these wonderful architectural monuments. They have more ornamental facades or face of the buildings, octagonal and better proportioned pillars. The pillars are supported by sitting lions. The examples of this style of architecture are five *rathas* at Mahaballipuram also popularly known as *Panchapanadava rathas*. The mandapas contain beautiful sculptures on its walls. The most popular of these mandapas are Mahishasuramardhini Mandapa, Tirumurthi Mandapam and Varaha Madapam.

(c) **Rajsimha Style**: The temples are made of bricks and stone and lofty towers rise tiers like pyramids. The examples of this style are structural Shore temple at Mahaballipuram and Kailashanath temple at Kanchi. They represent more elaborate and well evolved Pallava art. The Kailashanatha temple at Kanchi is the greatest architectural masterpiece of the Pallava art.

Shore temple, Mahaballipuram

Courtesy ASI .

(d) **Aparajita Style:** The last stage was named after the name of king Aparajita. The lingams are cylindrical and the capital is more ornamental and conspicuous. An example of this style is represented by a shrine at Bahur near Pondicherry.

Thus, the Pallava age witnessed growth in all aspects of life. Both Sanskrit and Tamil literatures flourished, it also saw the growth of fine arts, particularly that of architecture, and Hindu religion and economic prosperity also. Besides, the Pallavas contributed to the progress of Indian culture in the countries of South-East Asia as well. Thus, the period of Pallavas has been regarded as one of the remarkable periods in the history of south India.

The Chalukyas

Besides the Pallavas, the western Chalukyas and the Rashtrakutas in the Deccan constitute important political forces. Both these kingdoms had their rivals in the far south, namely the Pallavas and later the Cholas. Their period has also been important in the history of India for their cultural contributions.

It is still true to say that practically the political history of the Deccan begins in the middle of the sixth century with the rise of the Chalukya dynasty. The Chalukyas played a prominent role in the history of Deccan and south India for about two hundred years from the beginning of 6th century A.D., after which the Rashtrakutas became powerful. The Chalukyas set up their kingdom in western Deccan with capital at Vatapi (modern Badami in Karnataka). According to Badami inscription of 576 A.D. the Chalukyas like the Brahmin dynasty of the Kadam has claimed to be Hantiputras of Manavyagotra. According to V.A. Smith, "the Chalukyas were a branch of Gurjaran invaders from Central Asia and hence they were of foreign origin". But the Indian historians believe that they were Kshatriyas of the north and their predecessor Hanti belonged to Ayodhya. Hiuen Tsang also lends support to this theory when he remarks that Pulakesin II was a Kshatriya by birth.

There were two branches of the Chalukyas who ruled from two different quarters at two different periods of history.

(a) Early Chalukyas ruled from Badami (Vatapi in Bijapur district, Karnataka) for about two hundred years from 543 A.D.-753 A.D.

(b) Later Chalukya rulers from Kalyani for another two hundred years from 973 A.D.-1190 A.D. In the intervening period, i.e. 753 A.D.-973 A.D. for about 220 years and their important dynasty of the south the Rashtrakutas held the sway and the Chalukyas were completely eclipsed as insignificant petty rulers.

A. The Early Chalukyas of Badami

The dynasty was founded by a chieftain named Pulakesin I, who made himself the master of the town of Vatapi in about 550 A.D. and established a principality of modest dimensions. He aimed, however, at more extended power, and is said to have asserted his claim to a paramount position by celebrating an *asvamedha*, or horse-sacrifice. The next ruler of this dynasty was Kirti Varman. He defeated the Mayuras of North Konkan as well as the Kadamhas of north Kanara. Kirti Varman (567-92 A.D.) greatly extended his empire at the cost of his neighbours. His brother Mangalsen (592 A.D.-608 A.D.) ruled for about sixteen years. He also extended his empire to some extent.

Pulakesin II (608-42 A.D.)

The most important ruler of this dynasty was Pulakesin II, who was formally crowned in 609 A.D. The Aihole inscription issued by him gives the details of his reign. The greatest ruler of the dynasty was undoubtedly Pulakesin II who ruled for about 35 years. He was the contemporary of Harshvardhan of Kanauj. He devoted himself to a career of aggression directed against all the neighbouring states. He defeated the Latas of southern Gujarat, Gangas of Mysore, Alupas of Malabar, Mayuras of north Konkan, the Malavas and Gurjars of Brigukacha. In the east he made himself the master of Vengi, between the Krishna and Godavari. But his greatest achievement was his victory against Harshvardhan of Kanauj in 620 A.D. This victory greatly enhanced his prestige and made him an undisputed master of the south. The rulers of Kosala and Kalinga became so terror stricken that they at once submitted to him. Pulakesin II established diplomatic relations with Persia also. It was during his reign that Hiuen Tsang visited the Chalukya Empire. The kingdom having enormously grown in dimensions, Pulakesin II entrusted the administration of the eastern territories to his younger brother Kubja Vishnuvardhana in about 615 A.D. The latter made some additions to his charge by conquests but he does not appear to have broken away from Vatapi. It was perhaps his son Jaisimha I who asserted his independence. Towards the south, Pulakesin II defeated the Pallava king and threatened his capital Kanchi.

All the southern kingdoms, the Cholas, the Pandyas and Kerala, as well as the Pallava formed an alliance against the Chalukyas but they could not succeed against the volume of Pulakesin II. Hiuen Tsang records that: "The inhibitants were proved—spirited and war like, grateful for favours and revengeful for wrongs, self-sacrificing towards suppliants in distress and sanguinary to death with anyone who treated them insultingly. Their martial heroes who led the van of the army in battle went into conflict intoxicated and their war-elephants were also made drunk before an engagement owing to his superior forces. The king Pulakesin II who was a Kshatriya by birth treated the neighbouring powers with contempt. Indeed his benevolent sway extended far and wide and his vassals served him with perfect loyalty." The last days of Pulakesin II were glorious and tragic. The Pallavas grew strong and paid off old scores under the leadership of Narasimha Verman I (625-45 A.D.). He stormed the capital Vatapi in 642 A.D. and killed Pulakesin II and the Chalukya power was broken. He was defeated because constant wars destroyed his 90 per cent war resources and he was unable to command efficiently due to old age.

Pulakesin II's Successors

For nearly thirteen years the Chalukya power, which Pulakesin had laboured so hard to glorify, remained inactive; while the Pallavas dominated southern India. He was succeeded by his son Vikramaditya I who proved to be a great ruler like his father. In about 655 A.D. he recovered his father's throne and captured the Pallava capital Kanchi. He reigned from 655-80 A.D. and then he was succeeded by his son Vinayaditya. He had to enter into long struggle with the Pallavas in which sometimes one side was victorious and sometimes the other. Vinayaditya was succeeded by his son Vikramaditya II (733-47 A.D.). He was also a great ruler. He defeated the Pallava ruler Nandi Varman and captured capital Kanchi. He was also successful against the Cholas and Pandyas. During his reign the Arabs who had established themselves to Sind in 712 A.D. invaded the Deccan but Vikramaditya is said to have defeated them and checked their advance towards that direction. Vikramaditya's son and successor Kirti Varman II (747-53 A.D.) suffered a great defeat from the Rashtrakuta Chief Dantidurga and the imperial dynasty of the western Chalukyas was then destroyed, though they continued as insignificant petty chiefs.

B. Chalukyas of Kalyani

The Later Chalukyas of Kalyani was another branch of the Chalukyas who established their supremacy under their great ruler Taila II (973-97 A.D.). It seems at first he was a feudatory of the Rashtrakutas. Taking advantage of the conflict between the Rashtrakutas and Parmars, he declared his independence and later on in about 973 A.D. killed the Rashtrakuta ruler Kakka II and suppressed the other claimants to the Rashtrakuta throne. In this way he laid the foundation of another royal branch of the Chalukyas popularly known as the western Chalukyas of Kalyani. He fought successful wars against the Kaluchuris of Chedi, Parmars of Malwa and the Cholas of the south. The Parmar ruler Munjo died fighting him. Taila II died in about 997 A.D. His two immediate successors Satyasrao (997 A.D.-1008 A.D.) and Vikramaditya V (1001-16 A.D.) however suffered defeat at the hands of Rajaroja Chola and Bhoja Parmar respectively.

Jayasimha II (1016-42 A.D.)

He was the next Chalukya ruler, who routed Bhoja Parmara but was in turn defeated by the Chola ruler Rajendra Chola I at the battle of Musangi. Jayasimha II was at first the follower of the Jain faith but later on he was converted to Shaivaism. His son Someshwar (1042-62 A.D.) waged successful wars against the Cholas and the Parmaras. He, however, developed friendly relations with Jayasimha Parmar and helped him to regain his throne, when it was threatened by the rulers of Kaluchuri and Anhilwara. It was Someshwar who laid the foundation of new town of Kalyani which henceforth became the capital of Chalukyas. After Someshwar's death in 1068 A.D. his eldest son Someshwara II (1068-76 A.D.) succeeded him but after a period of eight years he was dethroned by his younger brother Vikramaditya VI (1076 A.D.-1126 A.D.) who was undoubtedly the greatest ruler of these Chalukyas of Kalyani.

Vikramaditya VI (1076 A.D.-1126 A.D.)

Vikramaditya won a great name for his dynasty by his all round conquests and cultural activities. He defeated the Hoysala king Vishnuvardhana of Mysore and Rajendra Chola II and recovered some of the lost territories of his dynasty. He is also credited to have started a new era known as the Chalukyas Vikram era. The famous poet Bilhana and Vijaneshvara the author of the well-known work "Mitakshara" flourished during his reign. After Vikramaditya VI's death in about 1126 A.D. the Chalukya power began to decline rapidly. Many feudatory chiefs asserted their independence and in about 1190 A.D. Someshwara IV the last ruler of the dynasty was overthrown by the Yadavas of Devagiri, who ruled up to the rule of Khilji dynasty.

Conflict Between the Pallavas and the Chalukyas

The main interest in the political history of penisular India from the 6th to the 8th centuries centres round the long struggle between the Pallavas of Kanchi and the Chalukyas of Badami for supremacy. The Pandyas were in control of Madurai and Tinnevelly districts of Tamil Nadu joined this conflict as a poor third. Although both the Pallavas and Chalukyas championed Brahmanism, performed Vedic each other for plunder, prestige and territorial resources. Both tried to establish supremacy over the land lying between the Krishna and the Tungbhadra. This doab formed the bone of contention in late medieval times between the Vijayanagar and the Bahmani kingdoms. Time and again the Pallava powers tried to cross the Tungbhadra which formed the natural historic boundary between many a kingdom of the Deccan and the deep South. The struggle continued for long with varying fortunes. This long struggle weakened both.

The first important event in this long conflict took place in the reign of Pulakesin II (609-42 A.D.) the most famous Chalukya king. The court poet Rairkirti has praised him in the Aihoo inscription. He overthrew the Kadamha capital of Banarasi and compelled the Gangas of Mysore to acknowledge his suzerainty. He also defeated Harsha's army on the Narmada and checked his advance towards the Deccan. In his conflict with the Pallavas, he almost reached the Pallava capital but the Pallavas purchased peace by ceding their northern provinces to Pulakesin II. About 610 A.D. Pulakesin II wrested from the Pallavas the region between the Krishna and the Godavari (Vengi). The Pallava king Narasimha Verman (630-68 A.D.) occupied the Chalukya capital at Vatapi in about 642 A.D. when Pulakesin II was probably killed in the fight against the Pallavas. Towards the end of the century there was a full in this conflict which was again resumed in the first half of the 8th century A.D. The Chalukya king Vikramaditya II (733-45 A.D.) is said to have overrun Kanchi three times. In 740 A.D. he completely defeated the Pallavas. His victory ended the Pallava supremacy to the far south although the ruling house continued for more than a century afterwards. However, the Chalukyas could not enjoy the fruits of their victory over the Pallavas for long for their own hegemony was brought to an end in 757 A.D. by the Rashtrakutas. Chalukyas ruled for a long time.

Art and Architecture of the Chalukyas

The Chalukya rulers were not only great conquerors but also great builders and patrons of art. They were mostly Hindus by faith. They built a large number of temples in honour of Hindu gods Brahma, Vishnu and Shiva, etc. They developed the *vesara* (mixed of the Nagara and Dravida) style in the building of structural temples. However, the *vesara* style reached its culmination only under the Rashtrakutas and the Hoysalas. Some of these temples have life-like statues of these deities which are superb both in their design and execution. Some of the temples have been excavated out of solid rock; some are brick temples while there are others which are structural buildings of stone finely joined without mortar. The Vishnu temple at Badami, the Shiva temple at Meguti, the Vishnu temple at Aihola, the Shiva temple at Pattadakal, the temple of Kasivisesavara at Lakundi, the Mahadev temple at Ittagi and the Saraswati Temple at Godagare are some of the most important temples built by the Chalukya monarchs. Almost all the towns within the Chalukya Empire have got some remains of one temple or the other. Cave temple architecture was also famous under the Chalukyas. Their cave temples are found in Ajanta, Ellora and Nasik. The best specimens of Chalukya paintings can be seen in the Badami cave temple and in the Ajanta caves. The reception given to a Persian embassy by Pulakesin II is depicted in a painting at Ajanta.

The Rashtrakutas

The Rashtrakutas built an empire which in its days of magnitude extended from south Gujarat and Malwa in the north to Tanjore in the south. Their capital was Manyakheta or Malkhed near Sholapur. Several views have been expressed regarding the origin of the Rashtrakutas. Some scholars connect them with the Telugu Reddis, others maintained that they belong to *Kshatriyas* who gave their name to the country of Maharashtra, while still others maintained that they belonged to the ancient family of Yadu (Yadavas). Another view says that Rashtrakutas were *Kutumbins* or agriculturists in the Andhra country. But the most acceptable view is that they were head of district administration under the rule of the Chalukyas and their title was Rashtrakutas from which they derived their family name.

Dantidurga (753-58 A.D.) was the founder of the Rashtrakuta dynasty. He defeated the Gurjaras and captured Malwa from them. Then he annexed the Chalukya kingdom by defeating Kirtivarman II. His successor Krishna I (758-73 A.D.) was also a great conqueror. He defeated the Gangas and the eastern Chalukyas of Vengi. He built the magnificent rock-cut monolithic Kailasa temple at Ellora (near Aurangabad, Maharashtra). It is dedicated to Lord Shiva. V.A. Smith has praised the art of this temple. According to him, "Excavated out of solid rocks, the structure of this temple is undoubtedly the most marvelous architectural freak in India".

The next important king of this dynasty was Dhruva, a younger son of Krishna I (780-93 A.D.) who turned towards north India in a bid to control Kannauj, then the imperial city. He made the Rashtrakutas as the greatest power of India at that time. While the Gangas and the Pallavas in the South acknowledged his suzerainty, the mighty Palas and the Pratiharas of the North were defeated and left humiliated. Under Govinda III, son and successor of Dhruva, the Rashtrakutas absolutely became invincible. He achieved victories over north Indian kingdoms. They exacted tribute from the Pallavas of Kanchi and installed one of their princes on the throne of south Gujarat. Govinda III was succeeded by Amogha Varsha I, who had a very long reign (815-77 A.D.). He transferred his capital from Nasik to Manyakheta (Malkhed, in the Nizam's dominions). The Rashtrakutas in his time succeeded in checking the southern progress of Bhoja I of Kannauj. Amogha Varsha I was a great patron of learning and art. He himself was a great author and is said to have written "Kavirajamarga". Next in the line of kings was Amogha Varsha's grandson Indra III (914-16 A.D.). He completed the illustrious work started by Dhruva and Govinda III, by imposing a crushing defeat on Mahipala, the Pratihara king of Kannauj, and taking temporary possession of his capital city. The last important king of this dynasty was Krishna III. In about 973 A.D., Taila II, a feudatory chief of Krishna III, who claimed descent from the early Chalukyas of Vatapi, defeated and killed Kakka II (the last ruler of Rashtrakutas). He then laid the foundation of the empire of the Chalukyas of Kalyani.

Thus, the Rashtrakutas became a paramount power in the Deccan for nearly two centuries and then were destroyed by later Chalukyas of Kalyani.

Achievements of Rashtrakutas

The Arab chronicles wise us that the Rashtrakutas were quite friendly with the Arab traders who visited their empire. These traders were allowed to build mosques and follow their religion without any hindrance. It testifies to the liberal attitude of the Rashtrakuta kings. The Rashtrakutas became the dominant power in the Deccan and even made their influence felt in the north. Their political greatness was accompanied by achievements in other fields. They were liberal patrons of Sanskrit literature. They erected numerous beautiful temples all over the country. The most beautiful of them being the *Kailash* temple at Ellora. Amogha Varsha was himself a great scholar of merit. He was also a great patron of art and learning. The Digambara, or naked, sect of the Jains was liberally patronized by him. The Rashtrakuta rulers had maintained trade relations with many foreign countries and thus they enriched the country and made their subjects prosperous.

IMPORTANT QUESTIONS

1. Assess the significance of the period from 300 B.C.-300 A.D.
2. Point out the salient features of the administration of the Cholas.
3. Discuss the important featutres of Pallava art, architecture and literature.
4. Who were the Chalukyas? Discuss the achievements of Pulakesin II.
5. Discuss the salient features of religious life during 300 A.D.-750 A.D.
6. Discuss the contribution of south India towards Indian culture.

REFERENCES

Basham, A.L., *The Wonder That was India*, Delhi: Sujeet Publications, 2007.

Chaurasia, R.S., *History of Ancient India*, New Delhi: Atlantic Publishers, 2008.

Directorate of School Education, *Higher Secondary Textbook of Tamil Nadu.*

Encyclopedia Britannica.

National Institute of Open Learning, *E notes.*

Raychaudhuri, H.C., *An Advanced History of India*, New Delhi: Macmillan Publishers India Limited, 1978.

Sharma, L.P., *History of Ancient India (Pre-historic Age to 1200 A.D.)*, New Delhi: Konark Publishers Pvt. Ltd., 1996.

Smith, V.A., *The Early History of India*, New Delhi: Atlantic Publishers, 1999.

Glossary

Prehistory—that period of our past that does not have any written records.

Mountain pass—the gap between mountains which help in easy access to the other side.

Celt—a type of stone axe made during the Neolithic period.

Microlith—a small stone tool made of flint and a centimetre or so in length and half a centimetre wide.

Butt end—the handle end of some implements or tools.

Animism—worshipping of plants, stones and natural phenomenon.

Matriarchal—a social system in which female member is superior in the family/society.

Citadel—higher portion of Harappan towns located on the western side.

Ideograms—symbols or characters transmitting ideas.

OCP—ochre coloured pottery.

BRW—black and red ware is sandwiched between OCP and PGW, dated to roughly the 12th-9th century B.C.

PGW—painted grey ware, lasting from roughly 1200 B.C. to 600 B.C. (Later Vedic period).

Pastoralists—people employed in domestication of cattle for subsistence.

Patriarchal—a social system based on the supremacy of female member in the family/society.

Egalitarian—a society in which all people are considered equal to each other.

Clan—a traditional social unit, consisting of a number of families claiming a common ancestor and following the same hereditary chieftain.

Tribe—a unit of socio-political organization consisting of a number of families among whom leadership is typically neither formalized nor permanent.

Jatakas—Buddhist texts with tales related to Buddha's previous birth.

Mahayana—that sect of Buddhism which believes in idol worship of Buddha.

Hinayana—that section of Buddhism which adheres to original teachings of Buddha.

Nirvana—extinction of human desire.

Tirthankara—prophets in Jainism.

Digambara—sky clad, a Jainism sect which remains naked.

Svetambara—a sect of Jainism whose members are dressed in white cloths.

PMC—coins which are punched with various marks such as fish, trees, hill, etc.

Donee—a person who receives a gift.

Eulogy—a piece of writing in commendation of a person.

Laureate—a person who is honoured with an award for outstanding creative or intellectual achievement.

Nagara—style of temple making followed in north India.

Dravida—style of temple making followed in south India.

Vesara—mix of Nagara and Dravida style of temple making.

Suggested Readings

Ancient Geography of India, Cunningham.

The Pre-historic Periods in India, Part I—S.N. Chakravarti.

Prehistoric India—Stuart Piggott.

Mohenjodaro and the Indus Civilization—Sir John Marshall.

Ancient India—R.C. Majumdar.

Some Aspects of Ancient Indian Culture—D.R.Bhandarkar.

An Introduction to the Study of Indian History—D.D. Kosambi.

Asoka and the Decline of the Mauryas—Romila Thapar.

Aspects of Political Ideas and Institutions in Ancient India—R.S. Sharma.

The Social Dimensions of Early Buddhism—Uma Chakravarti.

The History of South India—K.A.N. Sastri (ed.).

Beginnings of South Indian History—S. Krishnaswami Aiyangar.